Discipline and / A Practical Guide
the Disruptive Child / for Elementary Teachers

By the Same Authors

The Effective Student Activities Program

Experiential Learning: An Effective Teaching Program for Elementary Schools

Successful Methods for Teaching the Slow Learner

Discipline and the Disruptive Child / A Practical Guide for Elementary Teachers

Muriel Schoenbrun Karlin

and

Regina Berger

PARKER PUBLISHING COMPANY, INC.   West Nyack, N.Y.

© 1972, by

Parker Publishing Company, Inc.

West Nyack, N.Y.

Library of Congress Cataloging in Publication Data

Karlin, Muriel Schoenbrun.   (date)
    Discipline and the disruptive child.

    1. School discipline. 2. Problem children--
education.   I. Berger, Regina, joint author.
II. Title.
LB3013.K35   372.1'5   72-5368
ISBN 0-13-215806-X

Printed in the United States of America

DEDICATION

We dedicate this book to the troubled and consequently trouble-some children, and to their parents and teachers, with the knowledge and confidence that many of these youngsters can become worthy adults because of the love-filled labors of those who sincerely and whole-heartedly work with them.

How You Will Benefit from Reading This Book . . . .

This is a book to really help you with your discipline problems—the problems encountered in every grade, even as low as the kindergarten. In fact, the sooner the need for wholesome discipline is realized, the better—for the children's sakes as well as for the teacher's. It is not a book of philosophy or of psychology, but of methods and techniques. It will aid you by placing in your hands the ways and means of working with your disruptive children. You will find procedures with which to experiment, if you are to reach these youngsters, and consequently to teach them. It will also help you, we believe, to understand them—to comprehend their needs, and to make yourself aware of their problems. It is this awareness of the sad fact that every child who is a discipline problem is a troubled child which will enable you to help and to teach him.

The format of this book has been chosen to aid you in finding the information you need quickly and easily. Chapters have been devoted to the major types of troublesome children—to understanding them and to coping with them in your classroom. First you will find material to help you see yourself as the leader of the class, the teacher. Next you will be given some insights into the problems children may be faced with (and often are) in their daily lives. You will then find many suggestions that will help you to work on solutions to these problems—whenever possible—or to live with them when solution is impossible. We cannot go into a child's home and rectify all of the evils found therein, but we can offer that child a place of refuge and comfort for five or six hours a day. Since it is essential that you work with the parents of the troubled boys and girls, we show you how to win their confidence and cooperation deftly. Chapters follow on working with the child who has learning problems, and with those who are quarrelsome or openly aggressive in their behavior. No theory here, but good, solid steps to take. Attention seekers may plague you; in the chapter on this subject you will find ways and means to satisfy the needs of this type of child. The problems arising with the hyperactive child, with the under-achiever, and with the non-motivated child are discussed. Other chapters are devoted to the child with difficulties at home, the child who has a phobia and does not come to school, and the child who isolates himself from the other youngsters. We deal too, with the physically handicapped child, and with the child of poverty. We give you information to help the child who unfortunately is a drug abuser, and the one who drinks. Far from rare, you may find examples of either of these problems, even in the second or third grade. Finally there is a chapter on the saddest of all the problem areas—the youngsters who are seriously disturbed, those who are mentally ill. These children must have special attention and care— and the methods to use are here.

At the end of the book you will find a questionnaire, which will help you to look at yourself objectively. This self-examination is usually difficult to do, but here it is simplified to the extent that you can examine the specific steps you have taken in helping the disruptive children in your class.

We are living in an era of social and educational revolution. Many of the new voices in education are rich in modern ideas, and are certainly worthy of our study and consideration. The "Open Corridor" classes are one example of such experimentation. The British "Infant School" is another, and there are hundreds more. All emphasize and re-emphasize the need for creativity, and for meeting the needs of the individual child. Concerning this there can be no question. Nevertheless, we cannot stress too strongly the concept that in order for children to actually learn, there must be a certain amount of structure in the classroom. Children cannot learn in chaos.

Every method, every technique is based on our experiences in dealing with children—as teacher, counselor, and administrator. The experience continues on a day-to-day basis. Every method, every technique is based on love and understanding. We try to help you to peer into the child's mind, into his life and into his environment. We try to help you to create a situation in which the troubled child—and every child—can learn. As a physician diagnoses a case, so we ask you to try to help the child to solve his problems by diagnosing them first, and then by treating them.

Perhaps the words which should reverberate through the mind and heart of the teacher as he or she deals with all children, and particularly with the troubled, and consequently disruptive child are these:

> Hostility breeds hostility.
> Respect commands respect.
> Love awakens love.

Muriel S. Karlin
Regina Berger

ACKNOWLEDGMENTS

We are indebted to many people for their assistance in the preparation of this manuscript. We wish to thank particularly the following:

Mr. Maurice Wollin, Community Superintendent, District 31, Staten Island, New York.

Mrs. Helen R. Harris, Educational and Vocational Counselor, Public School 82, Manhattan.

Mr. Norman H. Harris, Principal, Anning S. Prall Intermediate School, Staten Island, New York.

The Office of Education Information Services and Public Relations, Board of Education, City of New York were extremely helpful, with special thanks to photographers John Kane and John Fulner. Superintendent Jerome Kovalcik has always been most generous with assistance and advice.

Our thanks, too, to our conscientious typist, Mrs. Mary Davies, of Public School 39, Richmond. The long and arduous task of proofreading was done by Dr. Leonard Karlin, and Mr. Henry Karlin. Miss Lisa Karlin contributed several photographs.

We are also grateful that so many teachers and friends offered ideas and suggestions.

Above all, we are indebted to the children we are privileged to work with, and who are, really, the reason for this book.

Contents

*the Physically or the Poverty-Handicapped Child · Helping the Child
to Function in the Classroom (If Possible, Before He Becomes a Problem) · Supplying Physical Needs Through Social Service Agencies ·
Raising Self-Esteem · Making These Children Feel as Important as
the Others · Taking Trips to Broaden Horizons · Setting Up Projects*

*The Underlying Inadequate Personality—or the Experimenter · Rec-
ognizing the Various Types of Drug Abuse · The Open Discussion of
the Effects of Drugs and Alcohol · Becoming a Friend Must Be the
First Step · Referring the Child, While Working with the Parents ·
The Pleas for Understanding · The Bridging of the Generation Gap Is
a Must—and the Bridge Is Love · Educating All of the Children to
See the Danger of Abusing Drugs · Dramatic Education · Keeping the
Means of Communication Open · Children Who Drink*

*Recognizing the Child Who Is Really Disturbed · Bizarre Acts, and
How to Handle Them · The Frustrations of Working with Seriously
Disturbed Children · The Difficulty of Communication · Refer the
Child to the Guidance Department Immediately · The Importance of
Early Identification · Working with the Child in the Classroom ·
Make Coming to School a Privilege · Helping the Child to Adjust ·
Learn as Much as You Can About the Seriously Disturbed Child, but
Beware of Labels · Exclusion from School · Prevention*

*In Regard to Structuring Your Class Situation · In Regard to Devel-
oping Rapport with Your Children · In Regard to the Actual Learning
Experiences You Are Giving Your Children · In Regard to Teaching
Self-Control · In Regard to Developing Rapport with Parents · In Regard to Working with the Troubled or Troublesome Child*

ONE

Establishing Yourself as
the Teacher

This is a book about children and teachers, and the interpersonal relationships between them. It is based on communication and respect, love and understanding. It discusses the art of teaching and the art of helping children to learn. It is concerned with class control and class structuring. All of these factors are interdependent, for we believe that one cannot possibly teach without love and understanding—without communication and respect, and one cannot have these without the ability to control his class, and subsequently, to teach the children self-control.

We believe understanding and loving children is as necessarily a part of teaching as the oxygen we must breathe to keep us alive. The chapters which follow will help you to understand your youngsters—particularly the difficult ones—the disruptive ones— the children with problems, who become your problem children. We hope to give you insight into the lives of some of your boys and girls—so that you see the connection between the events shaping their characters at home, and their behavior in school. Hostility bred at home causes the child to be hostile in the classroom. An angry youngster may be furious with a parent, yet take out his rage on a classmate—or even on a stranger. The problems

17

your children may have are often deep rooted—and difficult to extirpate. But you can understand them, and from this understanding comes empathy and hopefully love.

The successful teacher has a love for people; people en masse, and people as individuals. There is no substitute for this. If you do not love people, and enjoy being with them, if they make you feel vaguely uncomfortable much of the time, if you realize you are afraid of them, teaching will be just a job for you—and possibly an unpleasant one. If you really love, your work can be a source of the greatest joy. Not every day. Not all of the time. But, many, many days—many, many times.

If you can honestly say to a child, "But I really like you. How can you disappoint me by behaving this way?" you are communicating with this youngster on a most important level. Who in this world does not, deep down, wish to be liked and loved? Love is different things to different people—a smile, a pat on the back, a wink. It is the sign of approval—such as the gold star you paste on a little one's paper. It is the words, "I'm proud of you. This is fine work," which you have written on a composition. It is the comment, "Very good," you make after a student answers a question. The need for love and affection is so great that infants, cared for but not loved, not held, not spoken to, are unable to develop normally. One wonders if any human being is able to survive if denied it. Your students, your children, need it desperately.

Unfortunately, love without knowledge of teaching is not enough. Teachers must know how to teach—how to hold the children's interest, how to establish a climate for learning—and how to teach their boys and girls self-control. We have personally seen young teachers enter our profession directly after graduation, filled with love for children—but lacking training. And we have seen them leave the profession five months or a year later disillusioned and, worse still, considering themselves failures. Love and skill are both needed—one without the other is simply not enough.

It is our aim to assist you in understanding children and to show how to establish a structured situation in your classroom so that children can and will learn. Call it class control, or call it discipline—you must have it to teach effectively. Let us start, then, with this as one of our basic assumptions.

UNDERSTANDING THE ROLE OF THE TEACHER

Achieving discipline and creating a climate for learning in your classroom is the direct result of the image you have of yourself and your role as a teacher, for these concepts govern the manner in which you function. Let us examine these concepts therefore, in the light of teaching in the elementary, junior and senior high schools. They differ considerably from those of the college professor, and from others working with adults rather than children. The role of the teacher, specifically what he does, will not be identical for every reader, but there are certain defined areas which will prove of importance to all of us.

/ Since the earliest schools, the prime function of the teacher has been to transmit knowledge to his pupils, to impart skills and to help the child learn to solve problems. This basic aspect of our work has not changed for thousands of years. When we use the verb "to teach," it is these procedures which are implied, for it is these methods which our society and every society since the Egyptians with their hieroglyphics, and the Greeks, Romans and Hebrews with their alphabets, have utilized. We are dealing with the transmission of knowledge which one generation has received or developed to another. Traditionally the teacher is the adult, the pupil the child. This is true today as it was in "olden times."

However, we, as teachers, have developed many new methods to transmit this knowledge, and to meet the needs of the children of today. We believe lecturing, for example, is highly ineffective. However, if we substitute questioning, even to develop new ideas, the lessons are far more stimulating, more problem solving in nature. Discussion, constantly, evokes thought. We can, and must, develop techniques which will cause the children to formulate truths for themselves, to have the joy and the thrill of intellectual discovery. We cannot spoon feed them at every turn.

In the schools of other generations, the teacher was an autocrat, who ruled by domination, and who was certainly not above the use of physical or psychological punishment. The whip was not uncommon, nor the dunce cap rare. Fortunately we have left this pattern of behavior far behind us, and have substituted other means of influence over children. It is these means which we shall discuss throughout this book.

No teacher, today, can rule with an iron hand. The day of the despotic teacher is long gone. But nevertheless every teacher must have control of what is going on in the classroom. He is responsible for teaching children—and this cannot be done when they are not paying attention and when the resulting climate is chaotic. The teacher must achieve this control through a number of devices, but, primarily, through being in control. He must be the captain of the ship, or the ship will founder, and fail to reach its destination. He cannot be "buddy," or "pal," nor a member of the group, a contemporary or peer of the youngsters. He may be their friend and their confidante, and share experiences with them. Hopefully, he does. But, if he does not feel he is the person in charge he can rarely, if ever, be an effective teacher. It is his task to structure the situation to see to it that he is.

Yet the teacher should not dominate the lesson. Nor does he need to. If he establishes routines, shows the children there is work to be done, and gets them started; if he transmits his feelings of expectation to them (that he knows they can do good work if they try)—if, in short, he starts the intellectual ball rolling—he can then play his role as each particular lesson requires. He can sit on the sidelines while children conduct a panel discussion, or have a youngster teach. He can have a child write on the board, or lead the class. But his presence, and the climate of learning he has created will serve to structure the situation in his classroom.

We all know highly successful teachers who, were one to visit their classrooms, would never appear to be working hard. Their children are. But these teachers often give the impression they are relaxed and enjoying themselves—and, of course, they are. This is possible because they have established the climate for learning. They have laid the groundwork and conveyed to their children the concept that they are there to teach, and, more important, the youngsters are there to learn. They present material the youngsters will enjoy—from the first day of the term to the last.

This ease, this climate is not achieved overnight. It requires much work to arrive at this point. How do they achieve it? They may work with the children, planning the actual lessons, and determining the methods to be utilized. The teacher may wish to suggest alternative techniques to the class, or he may judge which are more suitable himself. He sets up the routines, and he consults with the children to establish rules. He advises them of the school regulations. He asks for their opinions, and takes them into consideration. If they find a topic is boring, and so advise him, he develops a technique to vary it. If there are children who are preventing the others from learning, he works with them. But it is he, the teacher, who sets the stage, who creates the manuscript, and who directs the characters.

No teacher who cannot assume the responsibility for creating a climate for learning can be a successful teacher. No child can even approach his potential if discipline is nil. A class must function as a team, and, as with every team, there must be a leader. While, theoretically, this might be a youngster, practically, it must be the adult—the teacher—in this situation. He is, after all, trained for the task, as well as educated for it. He must know methods and techniques, and he must have an understanding, a feeling, an empathy, for children. He must be able to work with them rather than on them. But he must also be able to control them so that when they are presented with work to do, they will do it. How many times have supervisors heard the words from children, "That teacher can't control our class." It is said sometimes wistfully, sometimes in indignation, with angrier words, "Can't you do something?"

We know of one substitute teacher, who, misguidedly, allowed her class of one day to "do anything they wanted to do." She thought if they wanted to read, they would read. She put arithmetic examples on the board, and suggested any child so inclined might do them. She took out art materials, and physical education equipment. Even with second graders chaos ensued. At three o'clock, one of the little girls said to her, "I have an awful headache. Our teacher is coming back tomorrow, isn't she"?

When a person feels inadequate to the task he assumes, be it teaching or practicing medicine, sewing a dress or repairing an automobile, he will have to work hard to overcome the inadequacies, and to build a positive self-image. However, in order to instill confidence in others he has to appear adequate. He has to give the impression he knows what he is doing. In no field of endeavor is this more important than in teaching. To help you to feel adequate, we have what appears to be a rather simple suggestion, but one we have found works extremely well. Plan—plan your lessons, carefully and completely. Leave nothing to chance. If you are not sure of the amount of time a lesson will take, plan more material than you will need, but plan, plan, plan.

However, do not regard your plans as inviolate. They cannot

be. They must be considered by you as flexible tools which can be varied whenever necessary. Do not hesitate to change them as the situation changes. You decide on a debate—and introduce the topic. The children, however, don't seem interested. Change— either the topic or the technique. Perhaps if you presented more material (questioning the children as you develop it) you could generate more interest. Perhaps you didn't give them enough of a "tasting sample" to arouse their interest—your motivation was faulty. Try to determine why the lesson failed and change the plan. In your mind establish lesson planning as a law, and flexibility as an amendment.

In your role as teacher, you need to wear many hats. To gain and hold the children's interest requires you use as much dramatic ability as you possess and can develop, to present your lessons.

A teacher is, after all, exactly that—a person who teaches. And this is what the children want. They feel far more secure in a structured classroom than in a non-structured one. They resent teachers who do not teach them—and they can spot a phony after twenty minutes of exposure to him. They know we are paid to teach them—and they want us to do so.

It has been our experience that the favorite teacher is one whose class is structured, who feels comfortable and unthreatened, and can relax with his students. He is warm and interested in them— but this in no way implies he will permit them to waste their time or his. He has something of value to give them, and he presents it in as palatable a fashion as possible. This is where dramatic ability comes in. He knows he is adequate to his task, and because of his adequacy, he becomes creative and innovative.

We all are familiar with how deadly dull a class can be—with a teacher who drones on and on—without modulating his voice or modifying his ideas. We have all sat through hours of eternity waiting for a bell to ring. But no one wants to be a teacher like that! A person who is interested becomes interesting; if he is intellectually stimulated, he becomes stimulating. Therefore you need to know a great deal about the subject you are teaching. Even a simple topic can gain new appeal if you find something in it to interest your children.

It is necessary for you to have the children's respect, so that you can respect yourself. You earn this by being a professional, by considering your profession as one of the most critical in today's world, as it was in previous civilizations. You can never allow yourself to go down to the children's level; rather you must try to raise them to yours. In the matter of vocabulary, for instance, there are some educators who feel the children should be allowed to express themselves as they wish, using the vocabulary they have learned at home and in the streets. It is our fervent hope that you feel as we do—that when a child is entrusted to us, we will try, in every way we can, to educate him—in all the aspects upon which we can touch. If we adopt the philosophy we need do nothing other than allow the child self-expression, we find we are teaching him very little, and preparing him even less for his adult life. How will he ever improve that vocabulary if we do not teach him by example to enrich it? We do not mean to give you the idea that self-expression is not to be encouraged. It surely is! Every child needs outlets for his emotions—and we can and should supply them. Drawing, composition, discussion are but a few. But self-expression need not imply four letter words. Is it not our task to teach the child the means to convey his ideas in socially acceptable and beautiful terms? He will learn to convey them in other ways outside our walls, but if we do not teach him the traditional words, who will?

How do you see the role of the teacher? This is a most important matter—and we suggest you give it serious thought. Our concept is of a person who creates the climate of learning in the classroom, who achieves discipline through firm leadership, who feels adequate to his tasks, who is interested and therefore interesting, who is a professional in his approach at all times, and who understands and loves children.

WHAT, SPECIFICALLY, CAN YOU DO TO CREATE A CLIMATE FOR LEARNING?

Establish Routines

The first step for achieving discipline and creating a climate for learning is to establish routines. Children want and need them, for, in this way, we can give them a feeling of security, which is one of their basic psychological needs.

1) There are a number of ways in which this may be done:

- You may have set up your routines, your system of doing things, long before you meet your class in September.

- You may decide on a number of routines in advance, and work out some of them with your class.

- You may work out all of the routines with your class, based on the philosophy that any rules and regulations made by those upon whom they are to be imposed will be more effective than if dictated by others.

2) When:

- Best in September.

- Never too late—always well worthwhile. If you are having difficulty in the middle of the term, institute the routines immediately. They should help you.

3) What procedures should be routinized?

- Entry—it should be delineated exactly how the children should enter the classroom in the morning. Do they go to the closet to hang up their coats, or sit down first? Is conversation to be permitted? In regard to this, we believe it should be—until a specific hour, at which time it ceases.

- Hanging up clothing. Designate a specific place for every child's coat. Be sure to give the tall children the hooks highest up.

- Seating—Assign a permanent seat, and be sure this is accepted as permanent. We have found it worthwhile to reassign seats every ten weeks—putting those children who were in the back up front, and vice-versa.

- Determine as many actions as possible which can be routinized, and then stress the method decided upon. This cannot be carried too far. Giving out materials, collecting them, getting on line, leaving the room, fire drills are only a few.

- Have work on hand for the children to do—*at all times.* This is fundamental to establishing a climate for learning. We are, incidentally, not talking about busy work. The latter is deadly. But we do mean work with value, which the children will find interesting. You need a stock in trade—of exercises, and devices which you can use. For example, we've found children love to "Unscramble." Give them a list of scrambled words, and they must figure out what they are. (You must give a designation, or this is too difficult.) For example, the following scrambles are all states. Which are they? ZONRIAA, KYNOWER, BALMAAA.

Or, using a dictionary, how many words can they find with the ending, "ology." Have them list the words, with their meanings.

Start discussions of current events, or sports, problems or personalities.

Children will not sit still or be quiet if they have nothing to do. They need, indeed, crave, intellectual stimulation. A bookshelf with magazines and books can supply this—when they have finished the assigned work—or before the day's work has begun.

If they have nothing to occupy them, don't expect them to "behave." They can't and they won't. It is too much, really, to expect of healthy youngsters, full of life and energy.

Making Your Classroom Interesting

The best means of achieving a climate for learning painlessly is to make learning as fascinating as possible. Here are some suggestions:

1) Try to link your lessons directly to the children's lives. When the curriculum is unrelated, it becomes your task to make it meaningful. To do this, you, yourself, have to be aware of what is going on—in the children's world. For example, they are all very interested in drugs and narcotics. Lessons in this area can be given, tremendously successfully, to virtually every grade—from the third up. The topic may be considered, too, in every subject area, not just in science classes. This is timely and important. It's our duty to educate our children—and you will find them "all ears" if you gear your lessons to their lives. (Be willing, though, to learn from them, too. On many grade levels they will have something to offer you.)

2) Make it experiential. Instead of lecturing your children, have them doing things. Plan lessons that are active physically as well as intellectually. Don't discuss "the pulse" without having them take it before and after exercise. (Be sure no physician has ruled this out for a particular child.) Do a play. But do it in its entirety. Have the children write it, stage it and act in it. Even have them advertize, and create and execute the stage settings, and review it. This can be done in social studies as well as language arts. It can even be part of the science class. When a class project is decided upon, have the children complete as many aspects of it as possible.

3) Make it timely. Have your children read and discuss articles from newspapers and magazines. The amount of information to

be gained quickly cannot be overestimated. Don't you think, too, that children should be aware of the happenings in the world around them? So often they aren't. They should know, too, how to read for specific information, how to skim, how to find detail. What better way to teach this than through the newspaper?

4) Take them on trips.

The interest you can develop in connection with a trip is surprisingly great. Children love to go places with their classmates and teachers. Shouldn't a first grader who lives in the city learn what cows and chickens really look (and smell) like? Or a seventh grader see ships being loaded? The selection of trips is almost infinite—if you open your eyes to the possibilities.

Trips are motivational, as well. Even a very unruly class will behave if promised a trip. Used wisely, this device can be an excellent one for helping the children to develop self-reliance and self-discipline. Be sure you stress the rules of behavior before the trip. We were once asked by a bus driver, as we returned from such an expedition, "What did you do, lady? Chloroform them"? No, but they had been told, repeatedly, and at great length, what was expected of them.

Set Up Rules and Regulations

As we have said, children seek a structured situation. This is one reason they are so upset if their parents become divorced. They seek the security which structure offers, in the classroom as well as in the home. (Incidentally, children showing many behavior problems in school are often reflecting upheavals in their home life.)

To have structure in your class, you need rules and regulations. The school administration undoubtedly has established some—and these should be discussed, so that they are understood by each child. This is particularly important when they are new to the school.

We feel children should have some voice in the establishment of these school rules and regulations. This voice is generally through the General Organization, or through the Student Government. We believe the feelings of the boys and girls deserve careful consideration—and should never be ignored or regarded lightly. The same is true in the classroom. Have your children suggest the rules of behavior they choose to live by. Have them elect class officers to help in the observation of them. Do not try to override or dominate them—but do attempt to have rules and regulations established which will make life in the classroom more pleasant for everyone. A simple regulation such as having a monitor pass the basket around five minutes before dismissal, and having each child discard any papers on the floor or in the desk provides a clean classroom with a minimum of effort.

A rule such as the following is helpful to teacher and children alike. "Any member of the class involved in littering will be required to give up his opportunity to be a monitor for one month." This brings up the establishment of a monitorial system.

Every Child a Monitor

By establishing an effective monitorial system, you can accomplish a great deal. You will be relieved of many chores, and your children are anxious to do them. We know of one teacher whose desk was always beautifully neat. "When do you get a chance to put everything away"? she was asked. "Oh, I don't do it. My monitor does," was her reply.

Everyone of us needs to feel he is worthwhile and important, and a job gives status. A youngster can go home and tell his parent, "I am the blackboard monitor. Mrs. Jones needs me." Of course they are impressed. The key to this system, though, is that EVERY CHILD MUST HAVE A JOB. No child should be allowed to feel left out, and become a malcontent. Furthermore, you then have a very powerful weapon. You can threaten to take the job away. However, this deprivation is extremely serious. Never, but never, remove a child from his position without first warning him that you are going to be forced to do so. Use the threat of this removal. It is often enough. If you must do it, do it with obvious reluctance, because you have lost some of the control you were able to exert on this youngster.

Here is a list of the many monitorial jobs you can establish in your classroom.

1) Elect class officers. President, Vice President, Secretary, and Treasurer. Their duties will be outlined below.

2) Elect representatives to the General Organization (providing, of course, your school has such an institution).

3) Two attendance monitors—one to take the girls' attendance, the other the boys'. Have them place the names of the absentees each day on a list which they submit to you, and also on a corner of the blackboard.

4) One blackboard monitor—who erases the work on the board, when it is necessary to do so.

5) One blackboard monitor—who washes the board every morning.

6) One window shade monitor—who adjusts the shades.

7) One clothing closet monitor—who is responsible for locking the closets, and opening them whenever necessary.

8) Three distributing monitors—who give out paper, pencils, books or any other materials to be distributed.

9) One wastebasket monitor—who passes the basket around five minutes before the end of every period.

10) Two fire drill monitors—who help the class officers keep order during fire drills.

11) Two housekeeping monitors—who dust the window sills, keep the teacher's desk neat and the closets tidy.

12) One bulletin board monitor who will put up and take down displays.

13) Two library monitors—to take charge of the class collection of books and magazines.

14) Two plant monitors—to take care of the plants, and also actually plant bulbs, seeds, etc.

15) One fish tank monitor—to care for fish (or turtles, or other living things which should be kept in every classroom). Choose a child who is knowledgeable in this area.

16) Three supply room monitors—to report for supplies and carry them when necessary.

17) Three collection monitors—to collect papers, books, etc.

18) A class host, and a class hostess, to greet visitors whenever they enter the room.

There are other possibilities—but this list should give you a wide base to work from.

The tasks of the officers are a bit more involved. The President should take charge of the class when the teacher is not in the room, and assist if he is busy. He should go on errands when a monitor must leave the room. He should lead the class when they go to the auditorium, cafeteria, and during fire drills.

The Vice President should notify the office if a teacher is absent.

He takes the President's place, when the latter is absent. He is the last person out of the room during a fire drill, being responsible for emptying the room.

The Secretary writes notes, for the teacher, on the board. He helps with class elections, and he must telephone any absent pupil, giving him the work he missed.

The Treasurer collects all monies—for trips, milk, charity. He is responsible for keeping records. If a class is asked to collect money for a worthy cause, it is his job to encourage them to contribute.

If you establish this system, make sure you give the youngsters as much to do as you can. This is excellent training, for their future lives, but, more important, it serves very valuable purposes in the classroom. Among others, it makes the children feel needed. Use every bit of enthusiasm you can muster to sell the importance of the tasks, and they will be done well, making your life far easier—and theirs far richer.

Other possible tasks: Class artist, who assists the other children who have difficulty drawing. In the same vein, you can have class writers, mathematicians, readers, spellers, etc. There can be research persons—to look up needed information. The variety of monitorial positions is vast, relying on your creativity. In one class there was one monitor whose job it was to decorate the room. This child amazed everyone with her intuitive good taste and imagination. She relied on the seasons and nature for her sources, and from September through June the classroom was made attractive by leaves, shells, pictures, and branches of trees. Her mother thrilled to this aspect of her child's education. The teacher, too, was really happy, for everyone who entered her room "ahed and ohed."

Explaining Your Expectations

Call it faith, call it confidence, or call it expectation, but, if you expect your children to behave in an adult manner, and to do their work conscientiously, they will. If, on the other hand, you expect or will accept negative results, you will get these, too. However, be sure your children know exactly and specifically what it is you expect of them.

Many teachers are shocked by the poor quality of work and attention they receive from their classes. They lower their sights, and accept poorer and poorer quality, instead of raising those of their boys and girls. One of the solutions is the specificity we just mentioned. If a child is aware of exactly the type of work you anticipate he will most often do it. Be sure, however, that he is capable of handling it, and that he is reasonably interested in it. No child would read dull material if given the choice. Nor should he be compelled to do so. But, if your assignments are of interest to him and if your attitude toward him is sympathetic, his attitude will reflect it. Sympathy and empathy are the bridges bringing teacher and child together.

If you expect good work, and you get it, reward the child. How? By a word of praise and by giving him a good grade. If you feel he should do better, return the paper, so marked and have him revise it—and return it to you again. *Make constructive suggestions, not derogatory remarks*—so that he is aware of why he did not do well the first time. Always build up—never tear down.

The same basic principle works in regard to pupil behavior. If Johnny is told, "You're bad," he will be disruptive, to prove what is said is true. If, on the other hand, he is told, "I know you're trying, but I am sure you can do better," he has your expectations to work up to. Never label a child. As we shall discuss later, at great length, you will be trying to find out why he is misbehaving in order to help him to change his behavior.

Find something each child in your class can do well—and build on that. Not one or two children, but each and every child, for there are always one or two talented youngsters who do everything well. All of the others fall into the shadows, which is not desirable. Every child should do one task—even passing the basket or distributing papers. Be sure each feels your expectation of him —and watch him try to exceed it. One class was asked to raise $10 (for a worthy charity) and told we were sure they could do it. They made plans themselves, and executed them and they raised $30. This device, expectation, is not foolproof but it does work—a great deal of the time.

Teaching on the Children's Level

If your teaching is to prove rewarding to your students, it must start at their level, and progress upward slowly but steadily. If you do not start with them "with you," you "turn them off." Their attention disappears, they become bored, and our great enemy, apathy, appears. Apathy—an unawareness, a lack of caring, and a refusal to take part in the learning process; apathy can make your students virtually unteachable.

Photo 1. Girls love making huge paper flowers.

Without progress, without that moving forward, the result, too, can be apathy. The new material you will cover, the unknowns you will explain, the pleasure in learning you create can dispel the apathy, and turn your children into individuals really seeking to learn.

1) How can you determine your children's levels?

a) By diagnostic testing. Simple skill tests, for instance, can show you the deficiencies in your pupils' knowledge and the point at which to start work with them.

These tests need not be long, nor involved. Have the youngsters correct them themselves—being sure they know why they are taking the test, and specifically what you will do with the results. A diagnostic test may be used before every unit of work. For example:

Before a unit on the government of the United States:

(1) We elect a President once every _____ years; the Vice President once every _____ years.

(2) The laws of our nation are made by _____.

(3) The judicial branch of our government passes on the constitutionality of _____.

(4) The Senate and the House of Representatives together form the _____.

(5) We elect 2 _____ from each state.

(6) The seat of our government is in _____.

(7) The number of Representatives elected from each state is determined by the _____.

(8) The President and Vice President are members of the _____ branch of our government.

The responses to these questions will give you and your students a place from which to start—in their study of our government.

b) Having found the starting point, how can this study be made exciting?

(1) A trip to Washington, D.C. with tours of the Congress, the White House, the Supreme Court. Difficult? Of course. Impossible?—that's for you to decide.

(2) More feasible—divide your class into committees, each turning into one of the branches—the executive, the judicial, the legislative. Have the committees choose one child to be President, one Vice President, etc. This person will outline his duties, his job—as he sees it. You may wish to have a lady President. Why not? Or a President and a first lady. There are many senators, representatives and justices of the Supreme Court—so these pose no problems. You can have the children be specific persons —in which case they could write to the person asking his views, and discussing the school project with him. Or the children may be "The Senator from Alabama," or "The Representative from the 15th district, of Wyoming."

Make this presentation come to life by helping the children to obtain as much information as they can on the subject.

(3) A film such as "Mr. Smith Goes to Washington," might be worthwhile.

(4) You might ask your Congressman to speak to the class, at his office, or invite him to visit your school.

(5) The class might put out a booklet, "Government of the United States," by Class 6-319, Public School #3, Mainstream, U.S.A., in which each child outlined the office he "held."

(6) You may put on an assembly show, written by the class and the teacher.

This unit can be developed to include far more. It can lead into a study of our history, or the history of a particular section of the country, for example.

If you found your students knew the material in the diagnostic test, you might proceed, for instance, to local or state government. We have found this an area in which children are surprisingly uninformed.

c) We have illustrated the diagnostic test as it might be used in social studies. In language arts, you could determine much about the children's ability to write by a device as simple as this:

Place the following on the board or on a rexographed paper and have the children write it correctly:

Correct and punctuate this short paragraph. Make sure you look for many errors.

deer granmother

when i came home momy sed to me there are a packaje fram your gramma. i was happy i hopped it wuz a toi or a radio i shook it and tought before i oppened it. i yeled and shouted. wuz i wxcitted. thank yuz four de nis pajamis.

Your grandson,

tim

There are actually forty errors to be corrected. However, give the children three points for each one they spot. This does mean they can get a total of 120, but explain to them this is a diagnostic test, to determine where they make their mistakes, and not a test based on 100 points.

d) In mathematics or arithmetic, use diagnostic tests to really get to the level of each child's knowledge. Test to find out what he doesn't know—so you may teach it to him.

This is testing for the same reason a doctor tests—to make a diagnosis. What does the child need to learn?

Besides testing, you can find out how well your children can do the work you plan for them by asking questions orally. However, it is easier to be misled by this than by written testing.

We used a nod of heads, as well, asking, "Do you understand?

If so, nod yes. If not, shake your head, no." To foster honesty we told the youngsters, "If you don't understand, there are others in the class who don't either. You will be helping me with my work if you're brave enough to tell me you can't understand what I'm teaching." In this way we ourselves learn, and we help our children to learn.

As soon as the class is at all capable of handling it, we believe you can do much in this area with an individualized reading program. You may use texts or preferably books from the library, but, in either event, allow the children choice—and vary the selections. We know of one teacher who offered seventh graders the choice of "Black Like Me," among other books. One child read it, at the same time her brother, four years her senior was reading it. They discussed it—at length. The parents, and the seventh grader were delighted because the child learned much from the book—and from her brother. Her love of books increased a thousandfold. In the conduct of this program, the children read while in class. The teacher then has time to discuss the books they are reading with each child—individually. Each youngster also writes a short report (one to three sentences) which is submitted. (Three by five file cards are fine for this.) He also keeps a list of the books he has read, and the teacher may keep a chart showing the progress of each boy and girl in the class.

Dr. Jerome Bruner has said we can teach any material as long as it is at the children's level of comprehension. Many of the topics which are usually reserved for adults are fascinating to children, as well. The fields of archaeology, and anthropology, sociology, psychology are all excellent to utilize. For example, a child can learn to comprehend by reading about prehistoric men, or about other cultures rather than dull or insipid material. Bring in subjects which you find stimulating, and share them with your students. A class can do research and write compositions about the possibility of life on Mars and will enjoy them far, far more than writing about "My Favorite Aunt," or "How I Spent My Summer Vacation." And, they will enjoy reading their compositions aloud to their classmates.

"This is a far cry from improving my discipline," you are thinking. But it really is not. For the more intellectually compelling your topic, the less inattention you will note among your children.

We had invited a guest who was showing a film to our assembly of 500 eighth graders. There was a buzz, and I called for "absolute quiet." "Don't bother," he told me, "When this film starts, you'll be able to hear a pin drop." And so you could. The film was about a young boy's search for identity—and there wasn't a sound in the auditorium.

THE FIGURE OF AUTHORITY

At a time in our history, when we, the adults, are suspected of being overly-permissive, at a time when there is upheaval all around us, the teacher, we believe, must represent authority. His is, indeed, a difficult task, for he must be the figure of authority without being authoritarian. He must represent to his pupils the strength and the understanding of a person dedicated to his task— and unafraid of its responsibility.

It has been our experience, dealing with hundreds of children, that this type of teacher is what they want and need. Many, many times youngsters have come to us requesting a change of class. Perhaps three or four times this has been "because the work is too hard." Most of the others have words to the effect, "I'm not learning anything. The class is too noisy." When the discipline is lax and disorder is rife the children lose a sense of security. Upon investigation, we discover this is often true with only one or two teachers. (In the junior high, which is the grade area of which we speak here, each class may have as many as ten teachers.) These are the teachers who have not made themselves the authority figures in their classes.

If you do not give this matter thought, you can lose your position and your control without even being aware of it. It almost slips away, and you wake up to the fact that you can't teach your children. There are, unfortunately, some teachers who never admit this, even to themselves. They are lost, but, and even more important, so are their students. The teachers in the first category are infinitely better off because they are willing to admit the truth to themselves, and then, we hope, try to do something about it. *The will to be* the figure of authority and to put the energy into it contributes much to a person's becoming the figure of authority. It is what the children really want and need and should have!

As the figure of authority, you structure your class—the work to be done, and the time to do it. If you enter your classroom and find the youngsters noisy, get them started on work AT ONCE. You must have firmness and purpose in your manner.

In the beginning of the school year, most of the boys and girls will proceed to do as you say. If one or two do not, say to each one, "Come on, let's get started." Say it with a smile, but so that the child will know you mean business. If any youngster is permitted to get away with not working, the fat is in the fire. The next day there will be another slightly rebellious child and the number will usually increase as the term progresses.

If, when told to work, a child refuses, immediately find out why. At least 50 percent of the time, the response is, "I have no pencil." Or no pen, or paper, or book. It saves a great deal of time and effort to supply it. But with the words, "I'll lend you one today. Promise me you'll try to remember to bring one tomorrow." Say this pleasantly, lovingly, but with firmness.

Be sure the child returns the pencil or pen before he leaves your class. If not, the give-away becomes expensive. Yet it is far, far better to keep some supplies on hand than to have children not working and disruptive because they lack them. You may wish to have a "Pencil or Ball Point Pen Contribution Day" at the very beginning of the term, to build up a stock—if your system does not supply them. Ask the children to bring in any pens or pencils they can spare. This is very worthwhile. Note, please—it is always, invariably and without fail, the child who has no supplies who cannot afford to miss his work. He tends to forget them daily—and you must keep after him. As an alternative, you may have him bring the pens or pencils into school, and keep them for him in a drawer of your desk. If a child continues to be negligent in this matter, he can miss work day after day, and fall behind. The child whose family cannot afford to purchase the basic school supplies is the one who usually needs the work the most. Do not exclude him—or allow him to exclude himself.

What of the child who tells you, "I can't. It's too hard for me." Immediately, give him another assignment—one he can handle. We knew of one youngster (of supposedly normal intelligence) who had not learned by the seventh grade to write his name. His story is obviously a very sad one—but his assignment was writing one letter at a time—and he did finally manage to master his name—but not much else.

There may be a child who devastates you with the words, "I

don't feel like it." If he were to say it softly, it probably would not be so bad—but he usually shouts it. Or he says, "I ain't gonna"! How do you handle him? You will find your best technique is to take the child aside and ask him, in a quiet voice, "Why"? Almost whisper. If he refuses to answer, press it.

"Can't you handle the work? Is it too difficult"? (If the response is "yes," as we said before, alter the assignment.) If it is "No," pursue it further. "Are you bored with it? Is it too easy"? (Here, too, if the answer is in the affirmative, change the assignment.) Still negative? Then inquire, "What seems to be the problem? Can you tell me"? If the child can't, ask, "Are you feeling well"? Or "Is everything all right at home"? If after inquiring about everything, the answers are all negative, say, "I would be pleased if you started to work. Shall I give you a different assignment, or will you try this one"? You'll find 90 percent of the time the child will cooperate.

The key, however, is communication between you and your children—learning from them wherein the problems lie. A patient approach, a friendly smile is worth its weight in gold.

When one of the authors started to teach, she noticed, one day, a child sound asleep at the back of the room. She walked over, intending to blast him—thinking "Who does he think he is—sleeping during *my* class"? But something stilled her "hand" and her tongue. Instead she told the boy to wake up—and see her later. The subsequent discussion brought forth the information the child had been out of his home all night. He and his mother lived in a one room apartment—and the mother sent him into the streets whenever she wanted him out of the apartment. He had wandered the streets for hours the night before. On this day, the child just couldn't keep his eyes open. How could he be blamed?

CONCLUSION

Teaching is, too often, thought to be a one way street. A teacher must, of course, convey knowledge but he must be willing to learn as well. He must peer into the children's lives and problems, for it is this knowledge which will make his work more effective. Most teachers come from normal homes, where they have had the many benefits of intelligent, sympathetic parents (both a father and a mother). They have had college educations, have been habituated to attend concerts, the theatre, and the lecture halls. The vistas of intellectuality have been thrown open to them. However, not having endured the physical, intellectual or spiritual poverty which so many of their pupils experience, it is only through empathy and warm feeling that they can attempt to learn of the sad problems with which many of their children are unfortunately confronted. It is these very problems which most often cause the problems in the classroom.

The unsympathetic attitude of an arrogant teacher stands between him and the education of an unfortunate child. It was Tagore who said, "The great walks with the small. The middling stands aloof." You must be compassionate, and understanding, yet still be firm. You must be the figure of authority, yet not reluctant to show your love for the children, for this, in turn, will awaken their love and respect for you. It is this love and respect which fosters the wholesome discipline for which every teacher strives.

TWO

Recognizing the Children with Problems, Who Cause the Problems in Your Classroom

The purpose of this chapter is to suggest to you only a small number of the myriad problems which face some of your youngsters in their daily lives. We believe it is of prime importance that you become aware of these problems, for they may affect the behavior of the children in your classroom, causing them to be disruptive or disinterested, diffident or discouraged.

The child who wants the limelight may be one of ten in the family, often told, "Children should be seen and not heard." The hostile youngster, who fights at the drop of a hat or a word, may have had object lessons of brutality right in his own home, from a drunken father, or a sadistic brother. The little one who is unpleasant may be so because of hunger—physical hunger. The variety and number of problems which can involve children is, unfortunately, unending. These problems may be physical or mental, social or economic.

Our intent is to educate you to try to see the child with understanding eyes—with X-ray eyes, if you will, which enable you to look for the cause of his behavior problems. As a physician must first find the cause of a malady, in like manner the teacher must find the cause of the child's inability to adjust to the school situation. Once you discover the problem, you can work toward helping to solve it. Do not be misled. Many times you cannot do so—but you can show sympathy, understanding, love and affection to the troubled youngster—and his behavior in the classroom will generally improve. Have you never put your arm around a child's shoulder—a child who is having a temper tantrum? As you speak softly, gently and kindly, you can almost feel the anger drain out of him, and gradually, if you are highly successful, a smile may even appear—as if by magic. It is the Bible which tells us, "A soft answer turneth away wrath."

Let us then discuss some of the problems which all too often beset so many of our children. We shall divide them into various categories, for the sake of clarity, but you must keep in mind the factor that they almost always overlap.

CHILDREN WITH PROBLEMS

Physical Problems

One of the most common of problems is poor vision. Can the child see? A child who cannot see clearly may not be able to read. We know of one child who, when asked to read the first line on the Snellen Chart (the eye-testing chart most frequently used) said, "I know there is a chart on the wall—but I can't see it." Another child with very poor vision developed into a severe discipline problem as a result of her frustration. She couldn't keep track of her eyeglasses, and without them was practically blind. She then became angry and aggressive—and engaged in constant fighting.

Is there a hearing problem? Often a child unable to hear his teacher becomes disinterested in the work—"turns it off," particularly if he is imaginative. He easily becomes a "wool gatherer."

Is there a heart abnormality? Some children with this type of problem often become extremely fearful. However, at other times they ignore their condition. We witnessed a game which illustrates this. Two boys were playing "Open Chest." One called out these words, and the other had to cover his chest immediately—or he received a punch. The one who was the recipient of the punch was a boy known to have had heart surgery. Fortunately he did manage to divert the blow sufficiently so that no actual harm was done.

However, the teacher who witnessed the incident almost fainted. It happened so quickly she did not have time to separate the boys.

(Incidentally, paste a red star on the record card of any child who is a cardiac case, and in the roll book as well, to serve as a constant reminder of the child's condition.)

There is a sad case on record of an adult who spanked a child. While the punishment was being administered the child expired. The adult did not know the youngster was a severe cardiac case. Of course, we are sure no reader of this book would ever beat a child. However, the danger inherent in striking a child even once must never be overlooked. The old fashioned "boxing the ear" often resulted in deafness. We have many, many ways of reaching a child. Corporal punishment must never be used—for, under any circumstances, it does more harm than good.

Children may have epileptic or other types of seizures. Should you encounter this situation, of course, you would immediately call the school nurse, doctor, the principal or even a neighboring teacher. Epilepsy is not uncommon today among young children. If there is no other adult around, you may need to call an ambulance. Diabetic seizures, viral attacks and other illnesses are also encountered. Furthermore, by perusing the health cards carefully, you should be forewarned and forearmed. Also you are able to understand the child's problems and feel for him.

One youngster, a fighter and a bully of sorts, whom we know well, has one artificial leg. It was obvious that he was compensating, psychologically, by indulging in outbursts of hostility. By peering into his problems, by discussing behavior patterns and future aspirations with him, we found we could reach him and really communicate with him. How often we can channel emotions which are destructive into actions of utility. We have asked this boy to do any number of physical tasks—tasks we were sure he could handle—to give him feelings of adequacy. It works! You would agree if you could see the look of gratification that appears upon his face while he is complying with our requests.

Mental Problems

The statistics are almost incredible—sadly incredible—one out of every ten persons in the United States is—has been, or will be in need of medical attention for a mental disorder. The severest discipline problems that arise in the classroom are most frequently caused by this—the saddest disease known to mankind—mental illness.

So often teachers will note, "So-and-so behaves as if he is crazy." Often they do not realize they have hit upon the truth. Repeated bizarre actions on the part of such a child make it desirable to seek the advice of a psychiatrist. In some countries children are periodically examined psychologically if they show anti-social traits. These examinations begin as early as the kindergarten age. Some of our children require such examination and treatment too, but rarely get it.

Bizarre behavior may be self-destructive in nature. We've seen children walk on hot radiators, for example. Hallucinations are another manifestation of mental illness. Usually the youngster does not reveal them, but sometimes when the teacher has won the child's confidence, he is more likely to speak of them, and possibly help can be obtained.

Many mentally ill persons are more difficult to help. One handsome young man, six foot two, eyes of blue, whom we dealt with, constantly drew pictures of knives and daggers whenever he "doodled." His books, notebooks and desks were always filled with these sketches. He was even consciously aware of his desire to kill. In school he was, for the most part, withdrawn. It was obvious to all who came in contact with him that psychiatric care was very much needed, and was instituted. His ambition was to become a "mercenary"—a soldier who fought for the nation offering to pay the most for his services. He never made it though—because he met a violent death at the age of eighteen, in an automobile accident.

These are examples of the problems which may plague some of your children. They live with them twenty-four hours a day; and this includes the five or six hours they spend in school. They cannot possibly banish them from their minds as they enter the portals of learning and much of the misbehavior we see results from the troubled state of mind of the child. Yet most of the time the teacher is unaware of the turmoils through which the child is living. Such youngsters may try to work at the tasks assigned, but their subconscious minds are often focused on problems or events which occurred in completely different places.

Psychological Problems

Psychological problems can sometimes be incredibly severe and dismaying to a child. We knew of a mother who held her child, Bernadette, a gentle, sensitive girl, in an ice cold tub of water for fifteen minutes. This was a disciplinary measure the mother had taken because the little girl often "lied." The "lies" consisted of charming fabrications that the imaginative child created to enable her to endure the cruelties perpetrated upon her by her sadistic mother. This parent also hung on the wall of her living room, for everybody to peruse, a booklet which she called "Bernadette's Lies." In later years it became quite evident that the girl had a talent for writing, but somehow settling down to do serious writing was something she forever procrastinated in attempting, although she was anything but lazy. Is it far-fetched to suppose that the cruelties inflicted upon her in early childhood had left profound psychological scars that prevented Bernadette from developing her literary talent? One is reminded of Macbeth when he said challengingly to the doctor, "Canst thou pluck from the memory a rooted sorrow"?

If a parent or a teacher emphasizes a child's weakness or holds him up to ridicule or censure the child is not merely hurt at the time, but the psychological harm done might well become permanent. Not only has the adult created distaste for the classroom, the teacher and learning, but the psychological harm done can be indelible. Would he not be justified in entertaining thoughts of becoming a school dropout? Whose would the responsibility be?

Another case comes to mind. Elizabeth was a model, a commercial success who thought herself an authority on beauty. She once told her friend, Margaret, that she thought her homely. Unfortunately Margaret believed her. For a long time she avoided mirrors. One day, while attending a course in sculpture being given by a renowned artist, this distinguished teacher told Margaret that she was beautiful. "But my features are so heavy, and my skin so sallow," remonstrated the young student in despair.

"Your beauty is not skin deep," replied the discerning artist. "It comes from within. You are beautiful!"

That did it. Margaret no longer avoided mirrors. She made a careful study of herself and became a very attractive woman, much sought after. And the artist had not lied, for Margaret's face did have an arresting beauty.

This teacher of sculpture had completely changed the girl's life. Is it not a profound example of how seriously damaging even a casual remark can be, and how a teacher can nullify it by perceptive kindness?

Problems Caused by the Generation Gap

Let us believe William Shakespeare when he tells us that the generation gap can and does breed problems that can culminate in tragedy. Neither Romeo nor Juliet's parents had ever won their children's confidence, for if they had, the saddest of all catastrophes—the death of a beloved child—might have been avoided. The teacher in the classroom takes the place of the parent. Throw open wide the doors of your heart so that the children may enter without hesitancy, without trepidation and without fear of punishment. If they do not feel you are their friend, they may seek out other persons whose advice and influence might convert their lives into an unending nightmare. Can we overemphasize the dangers that could beset your children, if they become, for example, the victims of dope peddlers? Let the child feel that you, his teacher, will never violate his trust or confidence.

How can he be made to feel this way?

First, *by your manner toward him.* It should be warm and friendly but not that of a peer. Remember, you are the adult in the situation—but a friend, nevertheless.

Second, *by letting him know that whatever misdemeanors he may be guilty of, you do not sit in judgment upon him.* Although he may be punished for the infraction of rules, make him aware that you do not bear grudges. We heard one excellent teacher say, in speaking of a disruptive child, "I don't want him to think I am angry at him forever."

Third, *by peering into the child's life and becoming familiar with his problems and difficulties.* This action, per se, will probably awaken in you a warm feeling for the little offender. A teacher once told her supervisor that she actually wanted to give a little boy a spanking, but when she pretended to do so by putting him across her knee, she saw the threadbare clothing in which the child was clad. It was January. She did give him a mock spanking, but then went out and bought him a warm pair of corduroy trousers.

You can also bridge the generation gap by avoiding intellectual and spiritual arrogance. By listening with respect to the children in all matters, you can learn of their sets of values which often differ from your own. This does not mean that yours is necessarily better than theirs or theirs better than yours. Open, honest, fearless discussion will enrich both the student and you and bring you closer together.

Home-Oriented Problems

We have referred, in our other writings, to school as the "great leveler." Looking at a group of children, it is virtually impossible to imagine the problems confronting some of them. Yet, invariably there are a great many, for the difficulties besetting a family affect each member.

We know of one child who refused to leave the school building day after day. The custodian informed his teacher the boy was always there until closing time at 6 o'clock, Monday through Friday. The teacher, a lovely young woman, discussed it with the child. He finally admitted his parents fought bitterly, and he could avoid some of the battle scenes by remaining in school. His father worked nights—and left the home at 5:00 p.m. The teacher understood, and arranged with the custodian for the child to actually work for him during the afternoon hours.

Parents may fight, with one another or with their children. They may drink, and become abusive. There may be older siblings who are bullies. (One older boy, by his own admission, frequently threw knives at his younger brother.) Families may be broken up; or fathers desert them; financial problems may cause untold difficulties. You can, we are sure, add to this list, ad infinitum. But the point we must make is that you consider the children in your class carefully. If a child is acting up and is causing trouble, try to find out what is troubling him. Speak to him privately—making sure he does not think you are angry at him. He may be able to confide in you, but not necessarily. Don't feel hurt. He may not be able to express himself—or he may be ashamed to. Almost without exception, we have found if a child misbehaves, he has things "bugging" him. Unfortunately we, as teachers, cannot always help him to solve them. But we can try. And we must!

School-Oriented Problems

There are children who suffer from problems which we, as teachers, have inadvertently caused.

How is a child to react if he is made to feel inadequate? Yet this is done, unconsciously, a great deal of the time. If a child is given assignments, repeatedly, which he cannot do, he loses self-esteem and self-confidence. Since almost every teacher was a fairly good student in school, this concept is one he has never, or rarely, experienced. But think about the child who cannot write a paragraph well, is unable to read at a sixth grade level, and is in the eighth grade. How else, but inadequate, can he possibly feel? A child does not have to be called stupid to feel stupid. He does not have to be told he has a low I.Q. or reading score—he is aware of it. Because he experiences these feelings, he figures, "What's the difference? School isn't for me, anyway"! Then he proceeds to go in any direction he chooses—by misbehaving, by becoming a truant or by becoming apathetic, and just biding his time. Our task, as teachers, is to help this child to become, and to feel, adequate.

If a teacher is unpleasant, children develop anti-social feelings early in October. Until then, they have given him a chance to prove himself, but after a few weeks have passed, they know what the term will bring. Just unpleasantness is enough to turn children off; some, invariably, to become behavior problems. We sometimes give this situation the dignified title, "a personality clash," but frequently this is but a euphemism. We have heard teachers refuse to discuss grades, for instance, with students. Antipathy is immediately created, and with it, unhappy children—and problems. Any child is entitled to question his mark; his interest, in itself, is commendable. And why should a teacher reject this opportunity to communicate? The request is not out of line—the teacher's handling of it is.

PREVENTING CHILDREN WITH PROBLEMS FROM
MAKING PROBLEM CLASSES

Preventing Problems

Many classroom problems can be prevented by starting work
immediately. For example, when the children enter the classroom,
there might be a diagnostic test (on the blackboard, or on a chart)
that teaches while testing. A multiple choice test of the following
kind is very valuable in this regard. (The child should copy the entire statement, as well as write the answer.) Explaining this type of
test will help determine what the children know—and what they
need to be taught.

1) When you have a group of words that give you a complete
thought you have a _____.
         (sentence, question, phrase, preposition.)

2) A sentence that asks you something is called a
_____.
        (question, statement, exclamatory sentence.)

3) A sentence that expresses a command is called a
_____.
        (an imperative sentence, a statement, a question.)

4) A sentence that expresses strong feelings is called a
_____.
        (a statement, an exclamatory sentence, a question.)

5) We put a period at the end of a _____.
        (statement, question, exclamatory sentence.)

6) We put a question mark at the end of _____.
        (an exclamatory sentence, a question, a statement.)

7) We put an exclamation point (!) at the end of a
_____.
        (a statement, a question, an exclamatory sentence.)

8) A word that is the name of some person, place or thing is
called a _____.
        (noun, pronoun, verb.)

9) A word that takes the place of a noun is called a
_____.

(pronoun, phrase, preposition.)

10) A word that describes a noun or pronoun is called
_____.

(an adjective, an adverb, a preposition, a phrase.)

11) A word that denotes *action* is called a _____.
(verb, adjective, noun, pronoun.)

Work, on the material above should be started immediately. It gets the class in order. Then the work should be carefully discussed, with many examples of each item given. It is best for every child to contribute one of *each.* If they are unable to handle any particular question, it should be taught again and again until they can.

Initiating the work immediately quiets the class.

Having each child contribute makes each one feel adequate.

Reteaching a topic which was not clear shows the value of such work as a diagnostic tool.

When a child gets 100 percent, hang his paper on the wall. Give him well-deserved recognition.

This type of exam may be used as a pre-test—before teaching grammar, and again after the work has been taught. *Encourage each child* to strive to get 100 percent. Show them they can—if they pay attention. If they need individual help, give it to them— or assign children to work together.

Taking the Positive Approach

Another way to preclude problems is by avoiding derogatory remarks that will antagonize the children. For example, it is far better to say to a child, "Jim, you could add a great deal to our progress in learning, if you put your mind to it," than to say, "Jim, you've done nothing all term long"! for the noncooperative child is often day dreaming and if we awaken intellectual pride we might tap sources of heretofore unsuspected creative power. Think of the teacher as the Genie that lights the magic lamp of learning!

Awakening Social Consciousness

It is our feeling that, as educators, we must do more to awaken a social conscience and positive feelings for their fellow human beings in the mind of each of our children. We can do this most effectively by living it—by being actively interested in every youngster—and attempting to help him. Another facet of this education might be through the printed word. Beautiful adages that have stood the test of time and that are so desperately needed today, might be displayed for discussion in different parts of the classroom. For example:

Do unto others as you would have others do unto you.

Politeness is to do and say
The kindest thing in the kindest way.

Hostility breeds hostility; respect commands respect;
Love awakens love.

Courtesy of American Red Cross Official Photograph.

Photo 2. Doing a real community service.

The children might supplement these adages; magnificent lines from poetry might be found and quoted, and the children might compose some themselves.

The picture of great men and their unforgettable words might be hung on the walls of the classroom. A portrait of Lincoln, for example, and his famous saying, "With malice toward none, with charity for all," might be printed below the picture. A likeness of Martin Luther King and his, "I have a dream," can be displayed vividly for all the children to see. All of these can be instrumental in developing in youngsters a feeling of respect for one's fellow man.

In subsequent chapters, you will find many more measures for preventing troubled children from becoming troublesome.

EARLY IDENTIFICATION OF SERIOUS PROBLEMS

From time to time you will find you have children with serious problems. By identifying these children—keeping anecdotal records of their behavior—it is often possible to refer them for help. The results are occasionally excellent. It is the teacher's task to note the behavior, and to call it to the attention of the guidance counselor, or of the principal. Parents may be aware of the child's problems, but frequently try to push them under the rug. They may have noted that Mary goes off and sits by herself all the time, but thought nothing of it. We watched one family ignore the sadistic tendencies of their son—as he literally perpetrated cruelties on animals—such as electrocuting them. The child was six years old at the time—and they were sure he would outgrow this behavior. He did not. In kindergarten he stuck tacks into other children— tacks which he had removed from the bulletin boards. He continued this odd behavior until the matter reached a head—when he seriously hurt another child. Then psychiatric help was obtained for him.

Any unusual, strange or bizarre behavior is worth noting and recording. So is aggression and hostility. Be aware, too, of the isolate—the child who removes himself from the group. Another indication worth watching is the child who clings to you. In short, we suggest you keep a card file, of youngsters who may become, if they are not already, serious behavior problems. If the problem does not improve, consult both the parents, and the guidance staff to avoid its further development.

Keeping Anecdotal Records

If a child's behavior is repeatedly anti-social, it is worth both the time and the effort to keep an anecdotal record of his misdemeanors. In this way, teacher, parent and even the child can see what the specific weaknesses are. They can discuss them and corrective measures can be taken. On one occasion an anecdotal record disclosed that a little boy had habitually left his homework undone. When this was discussed in the presence of both the child and the parent, the youngster said that he could not concentrate after school hours because he was too lonely. This was a "latch-key" child. During the afternoon he was always alone—for both parents were working. The mother suggested then that he do his homework with a friend who was also in his class. The little boy agreed and because he was a better student than his friend, he came to enjoy the concerted effort; and his friend, too, benefited thereby.

In keeping this type of record, the following form is suggested. Date, Incident (stated briefly) and Action Taken by the Teacher:

> 5/12   James threw papers around the room. I asked him to pick them up. He refused. We discussed this and he finally agreed and picked them up. Signed: _____.

A simple written statement such as this, of each incident, can be of help if the child needs assistance from the guidance staff. It also can help the child, and the teacher to see the progress being made. Often there are youngsters who, at the beginning of the year, have frequent notations but who, as the year goes on, have fewer and fewer.

CONCLUSION

We have indicated some of the problems which may confront the children we teach, and which may cause them to become disorderly, or downright menacing. The root of much classroom disruption often lies in the home situation of the disruptive child, or he may be difficult to teach because of a physical or mental problem. His lack of cooperation may stem from something which happened to him in school years before, or because he is in an uncomfortable situation now. He may be plagued by deep psychological troubles, or difficulties caused by society. For whatever reason, when we have a child who is misbehaving, we must try to determine the causes of his behavior—try to understand his trouble and to empathize with him. A child who has temper tantrums has them because he has so much inner rage he can no longer cope with it—and it spills out. Yet an understanding teacher can help him to handle these feelings, and can reassure him—so that he learns to cope with his emotions. Children are rarely, if ever, mean. They do the things they do for reasons of their own. It helps us, as teachers, if we can become aware of these reasons. Wherever there is a problem we can help to solve, without exception, we must try to do so. But even in the situations when there is little we can do, we can prevent the child from "taking it out on us, in school" by listening sympathetically to him, by accepting him, and by showing him love and affection. Easier said than done, of course, but still necessary—and still extremely gratifying. In dealing with troubled children, we often take two steps forward, and then one back. Sometimes it's two forward and three back. But eventually, except with the very ill, with the really sick children, we do make progress—and we can help troubled youngsters to be less troubled—and less troublesome. For the child with problems, love is the gentlest and greatest of all disciplinarians.

THREE

Basic Methods for Working with Children with Problems— The Troubled Children

In this chapter we are going to outline some of the methods for working with troubled children which we have found to be most effective in the years we have spent working with young people. There are some children with whom there is virtually no method which will work, for these children are seriously ill, and cannot function in a classroom situation. Fortunately, however, they are relatively few in number, and not too often encountered. 99 and 9/10ths percent of the young people you will have as students will not fall into that category. This is not to say they will be easy to work with, but they will be "reachable" and, if you have a number of methods at your disposal, you will be able to reach them. These techniques are not tricks or gimmicks, but procedures based on sound psychological principles. Many are obvious and yet we know from experience are not utilized by some teachers. But following a method is not enough. You must be humanitarian, interested in your fellow man—on a philosophical basis—and interested in his offspring on a practical and loving basis. If you hate children, as the late W. C. Fields used to profess, you should not be in teaching. If you are indifferent to them, you do not belong in teaching. Ours is a profession which must be based on love, for without it, our efforts are worth nothing. In dealing with a troubled child, one who annoys or harasses you or others, one who is hostile and aggressive, one who takes up an inordinate amount of time and attention, we are asking you to love that child, and to try the methods which we shall outline, basing them, always, on love.

Developing Rapport

When we mention "rapport," we are referring to a close, sympathetic relationship, and it is just such a relationship which a teacher should seek to develop with each of his pupils. This is possible when he teaches thirty or even thirty-five children, but difficult when he is in the upper grades, and has one hundred or more in his various classes. However, when there are troubled (and troublesome) children in any class, establishing rapport with them is one of the most important methods for helping them to improve, and to achieve self-control.

How can you develop this rapport, this closeness? Arrange to sit down and talk to, and more important, listen to this child. Not while the rest of the class is working, but at a time when they are not around. Perhaps you can have breakfast together, or lunch, or an after-school snack, or meet with the child during an unassigned period. "What," you are saying, "I'm supposed to spend my free time talking to *that* child"? Yes, that is exactly what we are saying —for this is absolutely the most effective method for reaching troubled children. They are aware of the fact that you are giving of your free time to talk with them. (Don't arrange this immediately after the child has misbehaved—because he will feel he is being rewarded for bad behavior. Do it, rather, between incidents.) When you have set up the situation, you can open the interview by saying gently, "We seem to be having our ups and downs, don't we? Why is it we can't get along? What can we do to improve things"? Sometimes the child will open up and talk to you. Other times he may not. But keep trying. Give him time to think and answer between questions. "Is there something troubling you"? you ask. Again, maybe he will tell you, but possibly he will not. You may continue, saying to him, "I can't understand it. I like you. Don't you like me? We're both here to work. You are here to work, aren't you"? (What child will say to you, "No, I'm not"?) "Why do you spend your valuable time disrupting our class? I guess you don't realize that's what you are doing." Always give the child an out, a way to gracefully back away from the situation. Show him you aren't angry at him, but perplexed. He is, you tell him, an intelligent child. Is there anything he is having trouble learning? Perhaps you can help him with it. Is there something bothering him—another boy or girl? Is there something wrong at home? By asking questions casually, by showing the child you really want to help him, by convincing him that you care about him, you can usually win over even the most hostile child. We have personally seen many, many children react favorably to this kind of treatment. They do not become angelic overnight, but their attitudes do change. It is human nature to be favorably disposed to someone who professes to love you, and behaves as if he does. Before the interview is over, get the child to promise he will try to co-operate.

Does this mean you will then permit this child to "get away with murder"? Certainly not. But, when he misbehaves, you can call him up to your desk, and whisper to him, "Oh, dear, are you letting me down"? This is particularly good if you have extracted that promise of cooperation. Usually the youngster will apologize. And, of course, you forgive him. Say to him, naturally and from your heart, "Honey, please try again—but this time, try harder."

We feel that affectionate names, if they are sincere, are one of your secret weapons. One of our favorite stories is of a young boy, seriously disturbed, who was sent to the assistant principal for discipline. The child was so agitated he could not sit down. "Come on, Hank, sit down." No response, but more pacing. "Please, Hank, sit down, so that I can talk to you." Still pacing, still angry. "Hank, sit down." Now the pacing increased in speed. "Hey, Pussycat, come here and sit down."

Now, not everyone can call a child Pussycat, and have it sound right, but this lady could. And, as with Hank, the response was almost always favorable. Hank turned, smiled, and said in an incredulous voice, "Pussycat"? but the smile told the entire story. The child sat down, and it was then possible to talk to him. And this was a very troubled, troublesome child.

If you can say "dear," or "honey," "sugar" or "baby," and mean it, you have it in your power to reach many, many children —even those with severe problems. If, however, it sounds artificial, don't do it. If you are too young, and there is practically no age difference between you and your students, don't do it. If you are a male, be careful which young ladies you say these words to, for adolescent girls can have fertile imaginations. But in many situations, where it feels right, this type of endearment can break down boundaries, and make children reachable.

Now let us consider rapport between children.

To develop this type of rapport in your classroom, a succession of lessons showing the necessity and desirability of good manners will do much to achieve this objective. We once heard a clever teacher tell her children the following story:

A famous movie star was asked why she had selected the man she was married to for a husband. He was not wealthy, not particularly good looking; neither was he an intellectual giant. Of all the men from whom she could have chosen, why this particular one? "Why, because he has beautiful manners" was the star's answer. "I mean the real thing," said the actress, "not empty gestures, but genuine refinement! I think really good manners are the expression of a truly kind heart, and this is the quality I need most in a husband."

Another potent way to build rapport is to fill the air and the room with sayings that make for harmony among the children. In this way, poetry can be put to very practical use. The children can find and compose appropriate sayings, and they might be hung around the room, or used as the nucleus of a composition or even a class play. The following is one that is particularly suitable for the classroom, for it is well within the range of the children's appreciation and comprehension:

Little Things

Little things, ye little things,
Make up the sum of life;
A word, a look, a single tone,
May raise or calm a strife.
Then, let us watch these little things
And so regard each other.
That not a word, or look or tone,
Shall harm a friend or brother.

The teacher herself must be a living object lesson of the attractiveness and desirability of good manners.

To further achieve rapport, encourage the children to be warm and friendly with one another—to help their classmates whenever possible. For example, the class artist can help the children who are less talented in the arts, while the class writer can be of assistance in composition work.

To encourage the children to learn and to help learn will not only foster the development of intellectual pride, but may also defeat animosities, preclude quarrels and make for harmonious relationships.

The children's birthdays might be remembered. A birthday song, a gift, a little party, all these expressions of good will will do much to create a family spirit, drawing the children and the teacher together in thoughtful appreciation and enjoyment of one another.

Children can be encouraged to listen sympathetically to each other's problems, and whenever necessary to enlist the help of the teacher in solving these problems.

We knew of a teacher, who won the affection of her pupils the first day of their being together by requesting each child to bring her a snapshot of himself. When the child was unable to do this, she took a picture of him, herself; then she pasted the snapshots on a piece of attractive mounting paper and tacked it to her desk.

These are but a few of the many ways that an ingenious teacher can achieve rapport among her children. Emotions can be channeled, love is fostered and a sympathetic relationship that may defeat ill-feeling and make for peace and harmony in the classroom can be achieved.

Showing the Children Love and Affection

"The origin and commencement of the malady is neglected love"! said Polonius, in speaking of Hamlet's illness. How many of our disruptive children suffer from neglected love? How many of them see object lessons of cruelty and injustice perpetrated at home? How many of them suffer blows and harsh words that damage their character and personality? If these children come to a classroom where the teacher is kind, gentle and understanding, this is the antidote she can give them; this is the object lesson she can teach them to counteract lessons in sadism they might have learned elsewhere.

Psychologists tell us that the love given a child will bolster him, and make him sturdy throughout his life. Ideally it should come from his parents, but here we are acting as parental substitutes, and any love is better than none. He will be better able to endure the whips and scorns of time that inevitably strike us all as we journey from the cradle to the grave. "Love," said William Shakespeare, "is an ever-fixed star, that looks on tempests and is never shaken." The teacher of today must endure many tempests and the love she feels and gives to her children will help her to remain unshaken. Do not be afraid to show your love for your children by a kind word, a smile, your arm around a child, a gentle voice, your sympathetic feeling when a child is in distress, lavish praise when he is endeavoring to do his job well, and a thousand other little gestures. A party now and then, your ingenuity in converting a dull drill lesson into a delightful game—all these undertakings will proclaim your love for your youngsters and because children almost automatically imitate, the spirit of love will become contagious and you will be building a class rapport that in itself is a magnificent lesson in social studies. A visitor entering your room will probably think or say, "What a lovely atmosphere there is in here!"

Treating Each Child Fairly and Equally

There are young teachers who are confused, and feel that love and firmness are conflicting concepts. Nothing could be further from the truth. You must be firm, and, as long as you are fair, there is no problem. You can be strong, and straight! If you say you are going to do something, you must do it. Children respect firm and fair treatment. They will not feel you do not care for them. Outward signs of affection and warmth will not make you lax. If a youngster can take advantage of you most of the time he will. But he will not love you for it—in fact he will be more likely to resent you for being "too easy." Make demands of your children—demand good work, demand good behavior, and you will get them. Love and respect your kids and they will love and respect you. Show them affection, and they will return that, too.

It is often difficult to show absolute fairness. Some children are so capable, that we get to depend on them. These are rarely the troubled children. The latter are usually undependable, and rarely asked to do any tasks, to be "monitors," and yet this type of attention is what every child craves. Therefore, try to avoid having "teacher's pets," and as we have outlined in Chapter One, give every child a task—for which he is responsible. Then, when a child misbehaves, threaten him with removal of his assignment. Don't take it away too quickly—unless the crime is great enough to warrant severe punishment. Make no mistake, this is strong punishment, for it is loss of status in the group, as well as the actual loss of the job. This is quite an assignment for you, the teacher—to create thirty or thirty-five meaningful jobs, but you can do it, using the positions suggested in Chapter One, and your own ingenuity. Try to give each child a number of tasks to do *daily*. Even if you rack your brain to do this, you will find it worthwhile—for these same tasks can be done by your class from year to year. Make each child feel needed, and he becomes far less of a problem. Many children have never had the "privilege" of being monitors, and the honor really influences their behavior. The work the children can accomplish is worthwhile as well. For example, we have seen many classrooms which are messy. Two boys passing the basket around cures this, and helps make them responsible at the same time. Or your classroom can be made colorful and attractive by bulletin board monitors. There is literally no end to the amount of work children will do if their energies are channeled.

But remember, every child must have something to do every single day. If you train the children during the first month to do their jobs, your work is infinitely lessened, and you have this powerful tool for control. Incidentally, change jobs around once a month, and each child can train the next one. This will heighten interest, provide opportunities for children to work together, and is thus good training for them. Class artists, class poets, class writers, class mathematicians can assist you with the actual teaching, if there are boys and girls in the class who are sufficiently proficient.

By making every child a monitor, you give feelings of self-worth to every youngster. We recall sending one particularly disruptive boy on an errand. Needing a monitor, we walked into a classroom and asked the teacher if we could select a child. She readily agreed, and we pointed to this boy because we knew him. As he rose, his almost automatic comment was, "Are you sure you mean me?" When we said yes, he squared his shoulders and came up to us—with very obvious pride.

Understanding Children; Exuberance and Misbehavior

At this point, let us discuss the rather uninhibited children who will sing or make noise, dance or "fool around" in the halls or when no work is going on in the classroom. For some teachers this is difficult to understand. Yet it may be nothing more complex than "joie de vivre," which, thankfully, these children have. If they are singing and dancing at an inappropriate time of course they should be stopped, but this activity should be scheduled for a better time. Why not the last half hour on Friday afternoon? Should you find your children behaving in this fashion, think before you take them too seriously. And "play it cool." Are they hurting anyone? Or are they just using up some youthful energy? Are they hostile or happy? There is a world of difference. They do not set out to thwart you, the teacher. They are not necessarily aggressive. The way to handle this is to find the proper time and place. Tell the children calmly and quietly, "We have work to do now, but we can sing and dance later." This can usually get them to stop the unscheduled activities. But who would not rather be happy than sad, dancing rather than working? Speak to them in a whisper, gently and firmly, and above all, without hostility. Don't erase smiles from their faces. You might even ask if they would care to teach the song to the class. (Make sure the lyrics are suitable.) Then devote five or ten minutes to it. After that, a resumption of work is usually far easier, and you, the teacher, have taken a giant step toward winning over the children. This is not to be done on a daily basis, but neither does it have to be a once-in-a-blue-moon event.

If you encounter children singing or dancing, or fooling around in the halls, treat it in the same manner—lightly. Don't make a federal case out of minor transgressions. (We are not even sure these are transgressions.) Children are young, healthy and full of energy, and life. They are not our adversaries. Why should we make ourselves theirs? "It's time to get to class, now," you say with a smile. They probably will smile back. If, on the other hand, you scream at them, they usually will scream back, and everyone becomes upset. *Judge what a child is doing, and handle the action accordingly.*

A case in point: One winter day, a serious, dedicated teacher, Mrs. X, came to the office of the assistant principal to complain, "I can't handle the situation," she said. "I need help. Immediately!" The assistant principal went with her to the "situation." About a dozen children were standing, talking, in the front hallway. They had been dismissed from class, and told to go home. They were not being disruptive, but they had refused to leave the building. Mrs. X had gotten frantic. Their reason for refusal was that they were waiting for their friends, brothers and sisters—and the temperature outdoors was 14°F. Mrs. X was so insistent on her "duty" as she saw it, that she lost her feeling for the children. The assistant principal sent her for a cup of coffee, and remained with the youngsters until they all left—voluntarily. There was absolutely no reason to send them out into the cold.

The next day Mrs. X told the assistant principal, "You know, I can't understand what got into me. I don't know why I behaved the way I did. Those children weren't doing anything to cause me to get panicky." She, herself, realized she had reacted badly, unthinkingly.

Today's children are far less repressed and more inclined to give vent to their exuberance than ever before. When it is out of place, it is our task to show them why. But we must talk to them with patience, and *without hostility.* Let us not make mountains out of molehills. Determine the cause of behavior, and if it is youthful happiness, don't extinguish it.

We, above all, must be thinking human beings, judging each situation as it arises. Children's actions should not be seen as threats to us. The youngsters are, or should be, our friends, our co-workers, our partners, and they should be treated as such. They can be a source of great joy—if we allow them to be. But, if we do not understand their actions, if we take them personally, if we are threatened by their youthful exuberance, we lose the pleasure they can bring to us. How often do we react to such situations because, we, ourselves, are upset, "up tight?" A bit of self-appraisal can really help us to judge ourselves. Let us recommend it.

Building a Success Pattern with Each Child

A child who is succeeding in his work rarely is disruptive. Try to build a success pattern with each child in your class. These few general rules might prove helpful. Of course you will vary them to suit the needs of your children.

1) Have the children draw or bring in pictures and charts to make the classroom enjoyable. Let it abound in colorful, attractive pictures and books (which you change from time to time), lavishly displayed in all parts of the room. Show the work of the children, but be very sure *every child is represented. Each youngster's talent should be recognized, and given full expression.* The perceptive teacher might discover talents that the child did not know he possessed. Literally cover the walls of the classroom with the activities of your children. In one prominent place, you might have a poetry corner, proudly displaying the work of your budding poets; in another, a small art gallery, where the accomplishments of your children who can express themselves in crayon, paint, charcoal, or whatever medium they delight in, are hung for all to see. Test papers which show high achievement should be given places of honor on bulletin boards. *Be sure that, in one form or another, the work of the troubled children is on display, for it is their work which is rarely in the limelight.*

2) Be sure your lessons are of value to every child. The intellectual food you prepare should be both palatable and digestible. Of course you will encourage freedom of thought and its expression. It goes without saying that cruel opinions should be labeled as such, but the opinion and *not the child* should be adversely criticized.

3) You can foster friendships that might help to solve some of the problems of the troubled child. By seating the children wisely —a slow learner (who is disruptive) with a bright child (who is not), much can be done to help the former.

Even if it were the bright child who was disruptive, the presence of a non-disruptive child with a disruptive one proves to be a calming influence. Experiment with this method—possibly changing the seats frequently.

4) Derogatory statements about the children should be meticulously avoided. It is much better to say to a child, "I know you can do better," than to say, "This work is poor," for the former statement is encouraging, while the latter is disheartening.

5) Encourage the children to ask questions, and to show you any work they may be particularly proud of. Walk around the room, glancing at each child's work. Troubled children respond

Courtesy Official Photograph, Board of Education, City of New York.

Photo 3. Puppets are for everyone.

well to this, for they often need attention, and need to build self-confidence.

6) Be extremely approachable to both the children and their parents, or to any other member of the family who is interested in their progress. Often it is an older sister or brother who shows this interest. You must give more of your time, your attention, and your patience to the troubled child, for he needs to achieve academic success—and if he does, very often this is the key to changing his disruptive behavior in the classroom.

Activities for Everyone

Feelings of inadequacy can make children misbehave more quickly than anything else. If you put an assignment on the board, and a child cannot do it, what is there for him to do? He may talk to his neighbor, or he may find other things to interest him. He may become frustrated and resentful. But, if he feels he cannot handle it, he will not even try.

1) Plan work in advance for every child, particularly for your potentially disruptive. The work must be geared to his level. If the class is reading, find material he can master—taking into consideration the fact that this is the eighth grade, but your problem child is reading on the fourth grade level. Do this in every subject area. At times everyone in the class can be given the same assignment; then individual planning is unnecessary. But at other times your specific preparation of work for each youngster is essential.

2) Find ways, too, in which each child can contribute to the class work. It is most important with the troubled child, who, psychologically, needs to make this contribution.

3) Give notes. Do not expect children to be able to take notes from your lectures. Most often, the troubled ones are the ones who will retain the least from your spoken words. If you place material on the board for them (and the entire class) to copy, you accomplish several things; you keep them physically active copying, you give them specific information to study from, and they have a notebook to show to their parents, and on which you may grade them. You do not have to write on the board yourself. It is better if you find a student whose writing is legible, make her the class secretary and have her take your dictation. This job will probably be a most sought after one—but the ability to write clearly is a necessity.

Trying to Determine the Basic Problem of the Troubled Child

When a child misbehaves, there is a reason, and if we are able to discover it, we can be of far greater help to him. There are a number of ways to seek this information:

1) Talk to the child. He may not tell you directly what is bothering him, but you may be able to discern where the difficulty lies, possibly by "reading between the lines."

2) Talk with his parents. Here, too, the information may not come to you directly, but indirectly. Furthermore, you cannot appear to be prying. Approach the parent with the attitude, "What can we do, working together, to help your child"?

3) Review the child's records—all of them—health, achievement, attendance, behavior, guidance. You may be able to find clues here. We recently discovered one very severely troubled child who had been "seeing double" for years.

4) Speak to the child's previous teachers, and to the supervisors who have worked with him. Has he manifested the same behavior in his earlier school years?

5) Consult with the guidance counselor, describing the child's behavior pattern. Working together, perhaps you can develop a method for teaching this particular child self-control.

6) In extreme cases, you may wish to bring this child to the attention of the assistant principal, or even the principal. They, too, might suggest approaches you could use with this youngster. The principal may also wish to be made aware of such cases, if the need for exclusion from school is a possibility.

7) You may wish to recommend the child for intelligence testing. At times there are youngsters who should be placed in special classes for retarded children, but who have not been identified. When you have a child who is inordinately slow, and who does not seem to be able to learn, request testing from the guidance department.

8) Placement of disturbed children in special classes is done in some school districts. If you have such a child, psychological testing is necessary. This is done through the guidance department.

9) If you have social workers at your school, you may turn to them if the child has a family problem—or a financial one. If such services are not available, speak to the guidance counselor, or to one of the supervisors.

Listening Carefully to the Child

Let the troubled child unburden his heart with words. A renowned psychiatrist once said the first thing a person should do when a problem is troubling him is to tell it to somebody. If a teacher listens with his heart, as well as his intellect, to a child's problems, much can be done for the youngster and sometimes severe problems can be precluded. A perceptive teacher once observed a look of misery upon a child's face, directly after the report cards had been given out. It puzzled her because the youngster's ratings were not poor, but merely passing grades. Touched by the look of desperation upon the little one's face, she approached him, saying, "What's the matter, dear"? The child burst into tears. An intimate discussion followed in which it was disclosed that the little boy's mother had said, "If you don't get high marks, don't come home"! Of course the parent did not mean what she had said, but the child had taken her literally. The teacher telephoned the mother, and, after a lengthy discussion, the teacher assured her pupil that he could go home—it was safe. It is entirely possible that a tragedy had been averted because the sensitive teacher had won her little pupil's confidence. How often are children's problems adult made, in one way or another?

Working on Solutions to Problems Together

If the child's problem is of such a nature that you can help him to solve it, this is a fortunate situation. For example, if his misbehavior stems from learning difficulties, it is indeed possible for you to work with him. Diagnostic testing is necessary to determine wherein his difficulties lie, and then special academic help is essential—given by you, by tutors or even by his classmates. If you find, as is often the case, a child who is poor in many areas, select one or two in which to concentrate your efforts. We would suggest reading and written English, because these are the most necessary for a person to function in our society. We would follow this with arithmetic help, as well.

When a child does not get along with other children, the teacher and the child can work on this. Often it is necessary to physically separate youngsters. If Mary and Johnny fight, put them in opposite corners of the room, after discussing the situation with them, and extracting their promise to refrain from quarreling, now that they are no longer neighbors.

Encourage the child to discuss his feelings with you. This may help, but far more often he is unable to do so, because he has become accustomed to bottling them up. If you encounter a situation you cannot remedy, seek help outside your classroom.

Seeking Other Aid if Necessary

There are many sources to which you can go for help with a troubled child. It is important that you and the child view this in terms of what it is—seeking help—rather than discipline. We have already outlined a number of sources—the child's parents, your supervisors, the guidance counselors, and social workers. If the

problem is a physical one, the school nurse, and the school physician might be the people to call on. Use your own ingenuity in
helping this youngster. He will be grateful, for he is probably more
used to punishment than to understanding, more familiar with
vituperation than with compassion. Seek help for him, and you, in
turn will be helped, for quite often his behavior in the classroom
will show improvement.

Stimulating the Children's Interest

You have a class which has a number of troubled children.
What do you do? For one thing, your teaching techniques have to
be particularly interesting, if you are to hold their attention. These
are the children who will not listen to you—just because you are
the teacher. They will go their merry way—unless you are able to
intrigue them—to make them sit up and take notice.

You realize they need drilling in arithmetic—but how many of
them will work at it? If you convert the drilling into a game—another reaction, entirely. Why not set up a World Series, and keep
the games running—getting a great deal of work accomplished.
Divide the class into teams, each with its share of bright and slow
children. Have the youngsters wear caps, make banners, decorate
the room, keep score on the board—and you can drill in every
arithmetic skill. Such games are often the answer to involving
every child in a lesson.

Trips are another method. "But," you are surely saying, "how
can you take a troubled child on a trip? He is going to spoil it for
all of the others." This will depend on the child. We have taken
hundreds of children, including many with problems, on trips of
all kinds, and have never had a child spoil a trip. Talk to them beforehand, really convince them, then make sure they realize that,
if they misbehave there will be no more trips for them, and you
will see that they will cooperate—beautifully. We know this from
personal experience. The troubled child wants to be included—tell
him you are willing to give him a break—but that he must not let
you down. He won't. If you feel apprehensive, keep him near you
—and he will even feel honored.

Do all you can to find unusual approaches to use in your teaching, and if you find your troubled children are disrupting the lesson, speak to them, explaining that you are trying to make their

Courtesy of Public Relations Department, The Empire State Building,
New York, N.Y.

Photo 4. Trips can serve many purposes. One to the top of the Empire State Building can be a never-forgotten experience.

lives interesting and showing them they are preventing you from doing this. "Do you want to do this experiment," you ask them, "or, would you rather not"? You can see what their answer will be; there is scarcely a person alive who is not intellectually stimulated by that word "experiment," and science is an area which can become highly motivational by virtue of the number of such experiments and demonstrations which you can do.

Discovering New Interests

James was the class nuisance. He was a bright child, but undisciplined. After his teacher had spoken to his parents, she understood this boy's problem. No one had ever said, "No" to him. What was she to do? The solution to this problem came to her unexpectedly. She was introducing the concept of the electrical circuit to the class, and James lit up, figuratively, not literally. It was as if there was a new world for him. Seizing upon this interest, the young woman asked James if he wanted to make a model of a house, showing the various circuits. Of course he did. Well, if James learned to show self-control, he could make such a model— working on it the last hour of the day. James was thrilled. He suddenly became aware of how disruptive he had been, and managed to work quietly for most of the day. Long before that project was completed, his teacher had several new ones planned. James made electrical games, and doorbells, burglar alarms and electric eyes. This was done under the supervision of a knowledgeable tutor, so that all necessary safety precautions were taken. He was asked to explain each project to the class, and did so very clearly. This child was almost transformed from an imp into a serious student as a result of a teacher's ingenuity.

But James was bright. What would you do with a slower child, who presents problems? Find something he will enjoy. It might be wood-working, or making model airplanes. (These do have a place in the classroom. A history of aviation through models is a most effective exhibit. Include rockets, and you have past, present and future.) One teacher was having problems with several young ladies, until she discovered their interest in cosmetics. She assigned, as their research topic, the history of make-up—a very interesting one for them. They then went into hair styling. Again, because they were intrigued, they were willing to work—and the projects were able to hold their interest. If a child has trouble putting ideas on paper, and research entails writing, have someone who is capable assist him. In this way, working in pairs can be very beneficial —to both children.

Making a Child Feel Needed

If a child feels he is a pest, he comes to school, but unenthusiastically. If he feels he is a good citizen, his attitude is entirely different. If he feels needed, he has a real reason for going to class. How can you make him feel needed?

We have already suggested establishing a full class monitorial system. Another is team work. By setting up academic teams, you can give each child a place in the class. However, the slow child might feel at a disadvantage. But if this team takes into consideration athletics, art, music, and every other skill—the child can contribute something. One enterprising teacher had her teams work in this manner: Each day there would be a new activity. For example, one week on Monday, every child who brought in a photograph of an inventor made four points. On Tuesday, every youngster who brought in a library book earned three points. On Wednesday, every child who received a perfect score in arithmetic made three points for his team. On Thursday, six points were given for a perfect spelling paper. On Friday, each child who brought in a flower or leaf received four points. The children never knew in advance which activity was awarded points or how many points they would receive. The class had been divided into six teams, and charts were made for each team. At the end of one month, the winning team went out for a luncheon party with the teacher. The class begged for the system to be continued. The second month the winners were invited to lunch at the home of the president of the Parent Teacher Association. This continued all year, and was completed by the awarding of prizes to the team which had the most winning months.

This teacher was a very ingenious person, and found projects which involved each child. No one gave up because the activity for Monday was academic. Tuesdays was sure to be something entirely different. When she asked for a drawing of a butterfly, almost any drawing was acceptable, and so, if a youngster was absent, his team lost credit. Attendance was very good. One mother telephoned to ask the teacher if she could please bring in her child's picture—the girl had a sore throat, and couldn't talk, but insisted on going to school. Should you try this technique, plan it carefully—and plan it for one month. It can always be extended, but only at the children's insistence. It may pall, in which case you need something else.

CONCLUSION

There are certain basic methods for working with children with problems. First you must be aware of the cause and effect relationship. Children misbehave for reasons, and if you can determine these reasons, you can sometimes eliminate the poor behavior, and help the child to develop self-control. We believe that the first thing any teacher must do to help a troubled child is establish a warm, close relationship with him. We use the term "rapport" to describe this. After you have developed rapport, you can sometimes determine the cause of the child's problems. Perhaps you can help to solve them; perhaps you cannot. But you can show the child love and affection, and treat him fairly and firmly. You can attempt to structure situations which will give the child some measure of success in school, and you can make that youngster feel needed and wanted. You can approach the troubled child with a view toward stimulating him intellectually and introducing him to new fields, new interests. Your entire approach should be a positive one, for, with troubled children far more can be accomplished with understanding and compassion than with punishment. A child misbehaves because he has not mastered the art of self-control. When you, the teacher, lose your temper, you show the child you have not mastered it, either. The young people have words for this—they "keep their cool." It behooves us to do the same, and to work with our troubled children, not against them, to show them we care for them, and are truly anxious to help them to succeed in this battle for survival which we call life.

In subsequent chapters, we will consider in detail the various types of children with problems, and some specific procedures for working with these troubled youngsters.

FOUR

Getting the Parents to Cooperate with You

Meeting Parents for the First Time

In our previous writings we have referred to the parent as the "essential ally." We suggest you adopt this phrase—and/or the philosophy underlying it—for, with parental cooperation, far more learning can be achieved by the child. This fact is taken into consideration and acted upon by many school systems in scheduling parent-teacher conferences early in the school year—usually in October or November. These conferences give the teacher an opportunity to meet the parents, and, under reasonably good circumstances, it should be possible to establish an element of understanding with them. This understanding can be phrased in this manner by the teacher: "Working together, you and I, the parent and the teacher, we can do a great deal toward helping your child to reach his potential."

Try to use this parent conference time, if your system has it, to talk with the parent of each child in your class. If you are in a junior high school, or in a departmental set-up, this is, of course, virtually impossible. However, it is essential that you make the attempt to meet, personally, the parents of any youngster who is not learning self-control, and not showing ability to work independently. The parents of these children are most often the ones who do not attend such conferences. In that case, invite them in by writing a note, or telephoning them. Stress that this is a first conference, and that you and they ought to get to know each other.

Discuss with every parent you meet, the concepts you are trying to develop with his child. Emphasize the fact that you are working with the youngster to teach him good work and study habits. These will, in turn, enable him to benefit a great deal more from every class he is ever in, every teacher he ever encounters.

Make each interview, even brief ones, very personal. Know some facts about every child and his work. "Mary Ann is so quick to grasp relationships between numbers," you tell her mother, as we did once. Her parent's reply was, "I've noticed that, too. I'm so happy you mentioned it. I've told it to her father many times, but he says it's only me, being a proud mother." But Mary Ann's mother realized the teacher did, indeed, understand her second grader's penchant for arithmetic, and a bond was established between them.

Don't ever start with a negative comment, for you will literally turn the parent against you, personally, and against what you say. Even words to the effect, "Barbara is doing an adequate job, but I know she is capable of much better work because I have seen glimpses of it," is better than "Barbara gets by. She's just passing." Follow up the first statement with, "She did a one paragraph description of her, 'Toys in the attic,' which was beautiful. Did she show it to you? But her next efforts at composition weren't as carefully thought out." By showing appreciation of the child's efforts, you make a friend, an ally, of the parent.

In this interview try to learn about the child. Has he ever been seriously ill? (This information may not appear on the health card —yet a child who has had rheumatic fever may suffer from its effects for years.) Has he problems with his brothers or sisters? (There are some families where children are fighting constantly. Often the children come into school very upset.) What is the parent's attitude toward the child? (Not all parents love their children—contrary to one of the great myths of all time. Child abuse is far from unknown.) You can't, obviously, ask a father or mother, "Do you love your child"? but you can listen to the parent, and if he or she does not, it will come out very quickly. We once were told, "I can't stand that brat. When I tell her I'm going to send her away, I mean it." And this mother did—four times—to mental hospitals—because the child "did not obey." (Children with such home lives usually respond to any love or affection from the teacher like a kitten lapping up milk.)

During the first interview, ask the parent if the child has had difficulty in his school work, from her own observations, and, if so, in what areas. Surprisingly, these difficulties may not show on the record card. Ask about outside interests, hobbies and pastimes. One teacher solved many questions he had about one of the boys in his class when he learned this eight-year-old delivered newspapers before he came to school in the morning. (Was it any wonder the child tended to fall asleep around 10 a.m., in the comfortably warm classroom.) This meeting with the parents should, in actuality, be a learning session for you, the teacher. However, so often, (we might even say most of the time) the parents we really want to see don't come in voluntarily. It's necessary to send for them. Let us suggest ways to do this:

> Requesting a parent interview (Compare these two notes):
>
> Dear Mr. and Mrs. Jones,
>
> I must see you in regard to your son, Edward's behavior. He has been impossible, and I am at my wit's end. Please be sure to see me tomorrow morning at 10 a.m.
>
> > Yours truly,
> > Mrs. Smith
>
> Dear Mr. and Mrs. Jones,
>
> I would like to discuss Edward with you. Could you join me for a cup of coffee? I would be able to talk with you next Monday at 10 a.m. If that isn't convenient, would you telephone me, please, so that we can make another appointment. I'm looking forward to meeting you.
>
> > Sincerely,
> > Jane Smith

If you were the parent, which letter would you rather receive? The question is unnecessary, of course. But let us analyze these short notes. In the first one, the teacher says, "I *must* see you in regard to Edward's behavior." She goes on to say "He has been impossible," and confesses, "I am at my wit's end." She shows her anxiety and her frustration. She then makes an appointment for the next day—giving the parents no alternate—and no recourse.

Supposing they cannot keep this appointment—which is really a summons—to appear. They feel uncomfortable, annoyed or angry, and threatened. What has Edward done? They conjure up pictures in their minds. Or they ask Edward, who immediately answers, "I didn't do nothing." Their anger or anxiety increases. They, psychologically, get ready to take on this adversary—the teacher.

Contrast this with the second note. Parents receiving it immediately think, "Isn't Miss Smith nice"? Why? She made them feel important. They have an idea there may be some difficulty, but the teacher is obviously a gentle person who is not threatening them—and they need not be on the defensive. The tone of this letter, and the welcome that is assured in it—will do much to achieve the aim—to bring the parent into the school. Should you need to write a letter to a parent, make it an attractive one—for never before, in the history of education, has there been so great a need to bridge the gap that has come into being between parents and teachers.

The same is true of telephone calls. Your voice, your attitude, your words—will reflect the feeling or lack of feeling you have for the child. As soon as a parent realizes that you do feel for his child and that you are interested in the youngster's welfare, he is partially won over—and his cooperation enlisted. Now, instead of one person teaching him, the child has two—parent and teacher. Try to meet with parents face-to-face, rather than discussing matters on the telephone, for the latter is rather cursory. This personal meeting should bring you and the parent closer together. It gives you the opportunity to learn more about the child, and about his problems.

Billy, aged ten, was a very disruptive child. He did little work in class, finding interests everywhere but in the lesson. A discussion with his mother disclosed the fact that Billy was constantly being compared with an older brother who was extremely bright. Billy felt he could not compete with this intellectual giant, and refused to enter into any sort of academic competition.

From the interview, the teacher learned that Billy played the piano (by ear) while his brother did not. She arranged to have him play every day, for morning exercises. The recognition he gained, plus the fact that he knew this privilege would be removed if his misbehavior continued, caused a marked improvement. His attendance improved, as well as his deportment, to the delight of both mother and teacher. He was needed, and this brought out the best in him.

Please check with your supervisor, to be sure you, the teacher, are permitted to write to or telephone parents. In some school systems, this is approved of, whereas in others it is the supervisor who must communicate with them.

Conducting the Interview

In any interview your first task is to put the parent at ease. Often parents come in to school in a highly emotional state. Part of it is a carry-over from their own childhood, when they were afraid of this figure of authority—the teacher. Part of it is with dread—what did Junior do now?

Be as nice as you possibly can. You cannot, after all, *demand* parental cooperation—you must *request* it. Muster up your charm, your tact, your interest in the child. If you are upset or angry you will quickly convey this to the parent. It is better to say, if you have a meeting scheduled, "Mrs. Jones, I'm afraid I'm upset today. Please forgive me if I'm a bit harsh. But I did want to see you about Edward." Then, try to be as calm as possible.

Take a positive approach throughout the interview. Begin by telling the parent as many good things about the child as you can truthfully say. Perhaps the child is warm and friendly. Is he fun-loving? Is he neat and clean? Does his appearance reflect the devoted care of his mother? (How heartening it is for the mother to hear this.) Is he helpful—does he wish to help you, or other teachers or children? Does he have leadership qualities? Any or all of these qualities can be pointed out—but only if they are true of the particular child. Mention as many of them as you can honestly cite. Do this with warmth and enthusiasm.

Then state the specific problem you are having with the child. If he is disruptive, ask him, in the presence of his parent, not in a derogatory tone—but in an honestly inquiring one—why he misbehaves. Some such questions as these might be put to the child.

"Jim, I feel you could contribute a great deal to our learning in the classroom. Is there some disturbing influence which is bothering you"?

The child will most probably say "no." Next cite his good points, and ask him, "Don't you feel you want to live up to your capabilities and help our class to be one of the best in the school? Now let's see how you can do this. You tell me—what can you do to achieve this"?

If the child can't answer this, continue in this vein, "Your mother and I both know you have leadership qualities. Now, wouldn't it be nice if you could influence the children to work hard"?

Before the parent leaves, extract the promise from the child that he will do all he can.

You may wish to give him a daily report card—which both you and his parents sign. Assure the child that, when he does his utmost, he will be commended for it.

It is well to minimize the fault finding, and emphasize what the child can achieve for himself and for the class. In this way the child is encouraged, and the parent heartened. Their cooperation is much more likely to be achieved than by invectives, unfavorable criticisms and name calling.

Put yourself in the parent's place. Would not this attitude on the part of the teacher be much more likely to gain your confidence and cooperation?

One very successful teacher approached parents of culturally disadvantaged children in this manner, "I can tell by looking at your child how hard you and your husband work to keep him so well dressed, and looking as nice as he does. Your boy must be very proud of you. Of course, we want you to be just as proud of him. By working together, I know we can achieve this. I know Jimmy will cooperate with us, won't you, Jimmy"?

Such words as these were the "open sesames" that earned the cooperation of the parent, and of the child, too, far more often than not.

Regrettably, we've heard teachers complain to parents, enumerating the child's "sins." This puts the parent and the youngster on the defensive—antagonism is born, and less than nothing is accomplished.

If a Child Needs Extra Help

There are instances when a child's misbehavior is caused by his inability to do the work required of him. If this is the case you may wish to ask the parent to work with him. However, the parent does not have to do this. You are the teacher, not he. Therefore, if you request it—make sure the parent realizes this is a request. Tell the person you will give specific assignments. Then do so. These need not be very complex—but they should be highly detailed—leaving no doubt in the parent's mind just what it is you wish covered. For example, "Read and study pages 110–118" is a poor assignment. A better one would be, "Read pages 110–118, and have the child answer the following questions":

1. Why did these events happen?
2. How could this have been avoided?
3. What were the results?

Please note: There are only three questions, but if a child is able to answer them, he has grasped the meaning of what he has read.

You can suggest to the parent that an older brother or sister might work with the youngster, instead or as well as the parent. This serves another purpose, too. It channels the energy of both youngsters, gets them working together, in a situation which can possibly prove beneficial to both.

When a child has caused problems, or is not learning, do not request a parent to see you unless you feel you cannot influence the child yourself. You can probably accomplish far more by privately talking with the child. However, if you feel it is necessary, write a note or telephone the parent.

Confidentiality

Before taking this step, be sure you tell the child you plan to do so. Sometimes just the warning may be enough to cause an improvement in self-control. However, once you have made the statement, if there is not *noticeable* change, you must go ahead with the conference. *Never, never threaten to do something and neglect to follow through.*

In taking this action you are using your "big guns." You have already tried speaking privately with the child, we are sure, not once but many times. While he may have promised you cooperation, it has not been forthcoming, and you have now decided to talk with the parent. Assure the youngster you will not reveal anything confidential he has told you. This may be very important to him, and your very mention of it serves to increase the child's respect for you. Needless to say, you would keep this promise. For example, let's consider the case of Betty Roves.

Betty's father drank, and she had confided this fact to her teacher early in the year. In spite of her sympathetic manner toward the girl, Miss Blank could not persuade Betty to lower her voice, and Betty tended to shout in the classroom, disrupt the lesson and be boisterous in the halls. Miss Blank had, indeed, worked with Betty many times. The shouting out continued, and, in fact, grew worse. One day Miss Blank told Betty she would have to see her father. Betty became abusive; her face flushed, and she appeared to be in a state of near panic. She could barely speak coherently. Miss Blank had not, of course, expected this behavior. When she took Betty aside to try to calm her down, the girl burst into tears. Further conversation revealed she had been terrified lest the teacher reveal to the parent that she knew of their family secret—that the father was an alcoholic. Once Miss Blank realized what the problem was, she promised Betty she would not mention this fact—and Betty gave her word she would try to control her behavior. She could not, however, and when the parents were interviewed, the confidentiality of the father's problem was respected. Miss Blank was shocked, however, when she met Mr. Roves. It would have taken a very poor observer not to notice his red face, and the odor of alcohol which was so evident. Yet, incidentally, the visit did help—possibly because the child's respect for her teacher was increased.

Do Not Make Value Judgments

If you must tell a parent something, be sure it is a fact, and not an opinion. Teachers sometimes may state their ideas as if they were undeniable truths—and this is surely not the case.

One ex-teacher told a parent, "Your son is lazy. He doesn't do a bit of work in school," thereupon the parent took from her purse some writing her child had done, and asked "What do you call this"? How much better it would have been had she said, "Your son has not been completing his work, lately. He sits and looks out of the window. Has something happened recently which has disturbed him"?

The child who appears slow may not be so—at all. Telling his parent he is can cause unnecessary pain. Instead, be specific. "Jeremy doesn't seem to care to read. He plays with his yoyo instead, while the rest of the class is reading." How would you react if you were the parent? Wouldn't you hurt? Or perhaps you as the parent might say, "Then take the yoyo away." But is that the answer? Hardly. Your task as the teacher is to try to determine why the child is reacting in this way. There is always the chance he may be bored. Bright children often become bored by some of the materials and methods we use. It behooves us to try to supply them with intellectual stimulation. We cannot place all youngsters into the same molds.

Talking to Irate Parents

How do you react when an angry mother or father comes in to see you (usually at your request, but possibly on their own). Do you respond by getting just as angry? That is, of course, the worst thing you can do. Let's discuss how you should handle the situation.

1. Say to the person, "Mr. Green, I'm glad you came in to discuss the problem. It's really important that I see you—so we can talk about it." Respond as calmly as you can, and as gently. Speak softly.

2. Listen to the complaint, and then say, "As I see it, this is the situation. Johnny was hit by a spit ball, but he was shooting them, too. I put a stop to it as soon as I became aware of what was going on. But I had to reprimand both boys."

Emphasize the concept that you try to be fair, and that you do not ever reprimand one child, and not the other.

If a child is hurt, the parent is usually more upset, more irate. Try to show him why the event occurred—*and reassure him that it will not happen again.*

The clue, in this situation, is a tremendously important one—namely that you do not react to hostility with hostility. When a parent is nasty, try to be particularly nice. Invite him to sit down, and to discuss the situation as calmly as possible. Even if he is upset, you have to stay calm. You are the teacher, and your self-control and poise are your most valuable attributes. If charges are made, consider them. Then refute them carefully. If you need records to back up your case, have them on hand, or get them—but use impartial, documented evidence whenever you can. Your tone of voice can act as a balm, or as an irritant—and with an upset person, obviously the balm is infinitely better.

I recall one case which literally made me lose a night's sleep. One young lady, constantly getting into difficulty, was chastized by the dean. To retaliate, she brought in her mother and grandmother, who were furious at the way she had been treated. The dean requested my assistance. We spoke to both ladies, and seemed to get nowhere, particularly with the grandmother. They left, both still annoyed. Several weeks later, the child was again out of order. This time she was leaning out of an open bus window. I called to her to move back from the bus window. She refused. I shouted. She remained there. Finally, I ran into the bus, and yanked her by the pony tail, just as the bus started to move. She was furious. She screamed at me, "Wait until my mother and grandmother take care of you." Since I had had the pleasure of meeting these ladies, I was quite anxious. The next morning the telephone rang. Sure enough it was the child's mother. Her first words were, "What did that impossible child do to get you so upset you pulled her hair"? When I explained to her what had happened, she said to me, "You know, after I spoke to you the last time, I knew it had to be something. I know you would never hurt any child. She won't give you a bit of trouble again." And, truthfully this child never did after that. Now a young woman, she comes back to say "hello" quite often. Her mother had understood what I had been trying to do—even that very first day. Grandmother, on the other hand, certainly had not.

Using the Telephone Effectively

We personally know of one young gentleman who started teaching in a vocational high school when he was twenty years old. He was younger than some of his students, and certainly the youngest member of the faculty. It was expected that the boys would give him a very hard time. Instead he became the most respected teacher in the school. He did this in one month. He spent hours on the telephone after school talking to parents. If a boy so much as called out, his parents received a phone call. In one month he did not have a single problem in any of his classes. This continued for all of the time he taught at that school. Once he had established this pattern, which was eminently fair, the boys came to respect and then to like him. He was also a very fine teacher.

There are those who believe this method to be an extreme one, but for this particular teacher, with his very unique problem, it worked. In many classes five or six calls may suffice. However, be sure that your approach is the guidance one. "I am sure," you say to the parent, "that you are anxious for your son _____ (the name is extremely important. It shows the parent you are talking about his child) to learn as much as he can while he is in school. I find he is not doing his homework, and I feel he needs this to reinforce the material he is getting in school. Could you or his father see to it that he attends to this? Thank you so much for your cooperation."

Referral to the Guidance Department

Very often you will find, in speaking to parents that just as you are having difficulty with the child in school, they are having difficulty with him at home. This family may be helped by the school guidance counselor, and possibly by the school or outside agency social workers. There are many situations with which trained personnel can deal quite effectively. One boy, whom we shall call Tim, was a poorly adjusted child, who would at times work very hard, and at others not at all. He would run around almost uncontrollably and yet sometimes sit and work beautifully. His family was referred to a social service agency by the school guidance department. An almost miraculous change took place in Tim. (It is devoutly to be desired that this happens every time a case is referred, but it doesn't.) Then, about six months later, the child reverted to his disruptive behavior. Upon questioning it was discovered his social worker had gone away on vacation. There was no one at home to control Tim. The social worker "father" had disappeared.

In homes where there is no male figure for the young boy to identify with, there is often a problem in school. The child does not know how to behave "like a man." Many times such boys will seek out male teachers or supervisors, with whom they ally themselves. These alliances are good ones, for the emerging man must learn from someone how to behave in the male role. It is hoped that the model chosen is a worthy one. Counselors are very often the male they select, and we have seen this prove to be highly satisfactory in numerous instances. The counseling situation is best suited to this, because the counselor can spend more time with the child privately than the teacher. He can assume the father image gently, but firmly. He must, however, be willing to do this, and be aware of what it is that he is doing. Lines of communication should be kept open, constantly, with the teacher—so that both are aware of the work being done.

Taking Early Action Before Really Disruptive Behavior Sets In

Many teachers, and particularly inexperienced ones, allow children to develop into problems in their classes because they are reluctant to take action as soon as a problem becomes apparent. This is unwise, for many reasons. Children must learn that no wasting of time will be tolerated. They must learn you, the teacher, are fair, but firm. Once rules have been set up in your class, by both you and the children, it is your task to see that they are followed. If a child breaks the rules, you must speak with him, and show him what he is doing. If he continues, you may wish to reprimand him more strenuously. If, after this, he is still not cooperating, tell him you will telephone his parents. If he still refuses, telephone them, or write to them, but in some way make sure that you communicate with them. Tell them, without hostility, why you are telephoning and request they speak to Johnny about his behavior. You tell them you are calling because you are anxious to get Johnny to do the serious work of learning, but that he is not willing to go along. You are not angry, you are not nasty, but you are requesting they help you, because Johnny will fall behind (or farther behind) if he continues in the manner in which he has been functioning.

We have heard parents say, literally dozens of times, when they are called in for pre-suspension hearings, "But why wasn't I told there was a problem? Why did it get this far? No one from the school has let me know what Junior has been doing." And their complaint is certainly justified. They have a right to know. It is true that, too frequently, both mother and father are working, and it is difficult to reach them, but a letter (registered) or a phone call in the evening often succeeds. These working parents are the parents who are particularly anxious for their children to do well in school. You are actually being considerate by notifying them, so that small problems do not become big ones.

We met one elected official, in a very responsible position, who showed us a letter he had just received from his son, written at the teacher's insistence, and mailed by her, stating the boy had not been doing his work, and was causing difficulty in the classroom. The gentleman was very upset by it. He was taking the matter very seriously, and was asking our advice—what should he do with his son? We asked if he had had time to talk with the child privately in the past few months, and he admitted that he hadn't, because he had been campaigning for election. We suggested that this become the first order of the day—and he agreed with alacrity. There are mothers too, too busy with their own pursuits to have time for their children. Sometimes poor behavior in school is a plea for their attention. Early action on the part of the teacher can at least bring this matter to the fore.

Seeking Medical Attention

There are times when you may wish to recommend the parents see the school nurse or physician, or their family doctor, because of some problem the child seems to be having. Children sometimes cannot sit still because of rashes, for instance (or tight underwear). They may be anemic, causing them to be lethargic in the classroom. When you sense there is something wrong, here, too, it is better to take action than to ignore it. Parents are invariably very grateful. Often problems of vision are discovered by the teacher, as well as those of hearing.

CONCLUSION

Parents should never cease to be your staunchest allies. In many cases the child does not realize that you can communicate with them, and that, once they are informed of the child's activities in school, they can persuade and encourage the child to cooperate with you, and to learn self-control.

In your dealings with parents, you must be extremely careful to be fair, and informative, for if you are hostile, you can accomplish nothing constructive whatsoever. You must work together to help the child, for, truthfully, in helping him, you help yourself. In speaking to the parents do not dwell on misbehavior, but try to show the child's good points, and his potentialities. Never speak derogatorily. Learn about the child from the parent, and establish a relationship with the parent so that, should you need his help, it will be willingly forthcoming. Remember you must request help from the parent, you can't demand it. Our motto, which we hope will become yours, as we have already said, is this, "What can we do, working together, to help your child"? Assure the parent first, "Should you have problems, perhaps I can help you with them. At any rate, I will be happy to try."

It is apropos here to speak of poet Bobbie Burns' magnanimous philosophy, "There is so much good in the worst of us, and so much bad in the best of us, that it scarcely behooves any of us to talk about the rest of us." Instead of enumerating the vices, let us emphasize and build upon the childrens' virtues.

If you use this approach, we can almost guarantee the cooperation of the parents.

FIVE

The Child with Learning Problems

The paper airplane flew across the room with amazing accuracy. It landed right on target, and the little girl's hand went up.

"Johnny threw a plane at me."

"Naw. I just threw it."

"You threw it at *me*."

"Nope. Can I help it if it hit you?"

"You threw it right at me."

"Naw."

"You did so. You didn't want to hit Miss Jones, so you aimed at me. I'm the farthest away from her desk."

"Oh, Johnny," sighed Miss Jones. "You can't afford to miss this work. You need this lesson so badly!"

How true! And what a vicious cycle! The children who need the work, who have the learning problems, are the ones who are inattentive. It is almost as if they haven't learned before, and they aren't going to learn now. What can we do about these youngsters—who have learning problems, but which manifest themselves as behavior problems; who interfere with the teaching; who are disruptive—and who, very, very often, not only rock the boat, but sink it, too? For the disruption spreads—from one child to another. A teacher who may have had one or two discipline problems suddenly discovers a whole class is unteachable.

What can we do about this?

First we must try to determine why the disrupters are disrupting. Wherein lie their problems? So often it is obvious these children are the poor students—the ones who are behind in almost every subject area. They usually have difficulty with reading and with math skills, and they have taken the attitude, consciously or subconsciously—I can't learn—so why try. These are children with true learning problems, who often become the disquieting element, the behavior problem in your classroom. And oftentimes the acts of misbehavior are the smokescreens behind which the child hides to cover his own inadequacies.

Of all the problems which face our children, the learning problems are the ones which we should be most concerned about—for two reasons. The first is that we can often help to solve them, by careful diagnosis and painstaking work. This does not imply we can work miracles, but we can effect changes, we can teach methods of study, and we can help the child to learn. The second reason we should be concerned about these problems is because our colleagues have helped to create them. Many, many times this has been unwitting and most surely unintentional—but nevertheless learning problems often stem from uninteresting teaching. If we can overcome some of the deficiencies evident in the child's educational background, if we can help him to achieve success, we can alter his whole life style. If we are indifferent to his learning problems, they compound themselves while he is in our class—and he leaves in worse shape than he came to us.

As educators, our prime purpose must be to educate our young people—to communicate with them, to give them information, to equip them for their future lives. The child with learning problems is the real challenge to us. Bright and even average students are able to learn with far less effort on the part of the teacher than their slower brothers and sisters. The slow learner, the child who suffers from a mental block, the child who is unable to progress in school—these are the youngsters who require extra effort from the teacher. It is essential to determine wherein the learning problems lie, and in what ways we can help the child to solve them. For what happens if a youngster is having such problems? As we have shown, he may become disruptive—the result of frustration. If the work is over his head, he may lose interest in record time—usually about ten seconds, and turn to his neighbor for companionship. He may carry on animated conversations or get into arguments. His entire attention is directed away from the work you are doing —for to pay attention may make him feel inadequate.

Often, too, children with learning problems try to give the impression which is exactly the opposite—and act like know-it-alls. We have seen children wave their hands violently, volunteering to answer questions—and when they are not called upon, becoming furious. Since it is not advisable to have any one child respond to all the questions, the reaction is almost inevitable. Sometimes, not always, this type of child is hiding inadequacy feelings. The techniques we suggest to help the child with learning problems are, we believe, valuable because they get at the roots of the problem—the child's feelings of inadequacy, and how to overcome them—how to help him to learn.

All individuals are different, and their learning abilities and mental capacities reflect this. Not everyone of us is an Einstein,— but nevertheless we believe one of the most interesting things about people is the difference—the individual differences among them. When children start school, not all are ready to learn. Many programs have been established to help underprivileged children in this regard—Operation Headstart being one of the finest.

However, when children start school, often the readiness is not considered, and the child is taught, but does not learn. The class masters its primer, but one or two individuals do not. The class progresses, but these individuals are left "at the post." It is here that very severe problems may be created. As the child moves upward through school he often falls farther behind his classmates, for learning is based on previous learning—and this factor causes many difficulties.

Learning Is Sequential

There are subjects in which a child may succeed if he is taught by a skilled teacher—science, for example, in elementary and even junior high school does not depend on previous learning as greatly as mathematics or reading. Neither do social studies—history and geography and current events—if the teacher does not depend on the child reading the text to learn the material. But reading, and other language arts, and arithmetic and mathematics are based, in great measure, on previous learning. If a child has not mastered the basic rudimentary skills, how can he proceed to other, more difficult ones?

We are firm believers in the teaching of reading through the use of phonics. If a child cannot sound out a word, and does not learn it "by sight" no amount of encouragement can get him to read it properly. If a little one has not mastered the concept of addition, how can he go on to multiplication? Yet we know children in the junior high school grades who cannot subtract. These are the youngsters who often become the discipline problems. Teachers try to urge them to study, offer them all sorts of encouragement— but don't actually teach them. A child who has not learned word attack skills, who has been subjected to only "sight reading methods" guesses, he attempts solutions, he tries anything. If he has been lucky he has realized that certain letters often have the same sound—and that he can take a chance on "into" sounding like "in." But when confronted by "instant" he is absolutely bewildered.

This child moves from grade to grade. He may even be held over. But unless he learns fundamental skills, he continues to fall further and further behind the rest of his group, and he becomes more and more discouraged in the learning process. He is also greatly handicapped because he cannot read textbooks—and get anything except a headache from them. Yet how often does the teacher give an assignment which relies completely on reading? The unfortunate child and his slow learning brother or sister, who can read the textbook with a bit more skill, but not comprehend it, how can they learn? The reading assignment is gone over in class but often superficially, at best. Then a test is given on the material —and the results have to be poor. For it is almost guaranteed— the child can't read the test. If the teacher reads the questions aloud, he'll do better—but this youngster usually cannot write well, either. His poor foundation is literally killing him and he becomes a discipline problem.

What can you do to help such children?

Establish Communication

1) Try to establish communication with the disruptive child. Arrange time to speak with him privately—and quietly. This should not be immediately after he has been disruptive, when you

and he may be angry and upset. Rather it should be after a good day. (Give this child special work he can handle, praise him for it —and you structure the "good day.")

Talk about the child's learning problems with him. Often he will be ashamed to admit them, or he will be unaware of their severity. Explain, however, that you want to work with him and help him, but that his progress will depend on him. It is essential that you get the child to realize you will help—but that it is his responsibility.

Use every bit of tact, of love, of affection you have toward the child. Win him over. He needs you desperately. If you convince him you care, that you really "give a damn" you have half the battle won.

Your own enthusiasm will be contagious. Your sincere desire to see him progress will be the springboard that will lead him into a desire to work with you, particularly if your attitude, your words and your manner are truly sympathetic.

While you are helping a child, he must never feel you are sitting in judgment of him, or blaming him for his inadequacies.

Remember, no child is perfect. The child will improve, will slip back. Don't worry. In time he'll make progress.

Explain that first you must find out what his specific problems are, and that you will use tests to determine them.

Write a note to the parents suggesting that the child be given a complete physical examination, including his hearing and his vision. Be sure, however, that he is taken to an expert who can check for visual perception difficulties. There are many children who do not learn to read because their vision is impaired, but this is not picked up by an examination with the Snellen chart. It requires a person who has studied this area extensively. Children may see only the first three letters of a word, or the last. They may see the letters garbled. One little girl read the word LEFT as FELT. This condition is not rare—but it is not common enough for it to be checked for routinely. Yet it has been a very serious problem in the lives of many people. Lucy Johnson Nugent is one of them. Incidentally, often the treatment for these disorders is exercise.

When a youngster has a learning problem, we must try every avenue open to us to discover what it is.

2) Then do your diagnostic testing to determine the needs of

the individual children. These tests may be the standardized tests used in many school districts, or they may be teacher made. The latter are good, or better, than the former. But this testing must be done, even in the junior high grades. When grading the tests, check the individual papers carefully. This is very effective if done with the child sitting next to you. Show him his errors, and work out a program with him. You may find not every child needs an individualized program, but many of those with learning problems certainly do.

To be more specific, even if you are teaching social studies, if you discover a child whose reading is very poor, work with him on reading skills as part of the social studies teaching. If possible, recommend help for him—in the form of special tutoring if it is available, or special classes. But be aware of his difficulty, so that when you are teaching the class, you do not expect this child, and others like him, to learn material from the textbook. It must be taught to him verbally. It must be made interesting, and relevant to his life. You will find that if you are teaching in this way, the child will often cease to be disruptive.

It is most important for you to work with the child, directly, on a one-to-one basis. To find the time for this, give your class some written assignment to do in class; we surely are not implying "busy work." But if you assign a composition, there is no reason why it may not be written in class, while you help individual children. The same is true of reading. Library books can be read during class time. In fact, this procedure is very valid, for you can structure the quiet environment which is most productive to reading, and you can supply books which the children will enjoy, thereby showing them the pleasures of reading. During the assembly period as well, or while your class is in the gym (with another teacher) you can do work with children singly or in small groups.

As you work with an individual child, such as our paper airplane designer, make sure you communicate with him. Let him know he has to fill in the gaps in his foundation, or he will continue to have problems. We have found that "leveling" with children, "telling it like it is," but not criticizing them, has a very good effect. "It seems to me, Billy," you say, "that at some point you haven't learned to pick out the ideas from a paragraph." (By the way, ask the child what is meant by a paragraph. He may not even know that. We have found that often children do not know words which are so much a part of our vocabulary that this seems incredible to us. One junior high school typing teacher told us that for weeks she had been saying, "We are aiming for speed with accuracy, but speed without accuracy is useless." She said she repeated this many, many times. One day she suddenly asked the class, "Who knows what accuracy means"? "Raise your hands if you know." Only half of the class knew. One wonders what the other half thought it meant.)

Returning to Billy, if he doesn't know what a paragraph is, it is a simple matter to teach it to him. Then show him how to select the main ideas. Give him work to do—you may even use the social studies or science textbook for this—and have him select the main ideas. Check his work to be sure he is doing it correctly. Then continue to see if he has mastered other reading skills.

One motivational device we have used successfully with children who have reading difficulties is making a tape recording of their oral reading. Explain you will hold this tape, have them make another at the end of the year, and then have the children themselves compare their progress.

You may wish to involve the parents or an older brother or sister in your work with the youngster. Invite the mother in to see you, and explain to her that you are trying to eliminate some of her child's learning difficulties. If you are able to, work out an instructional program in which an adult at home can assist the child with specific assignments which will reinforce the material you are teaching him. Just asking a parent to help, in the abstract, is never as effective as if you tell her you plan to send home definite instructions. For instance, a child may need to read aloud. Give him a note, with a particular story indicated, and several questions his tutor is to ask him. This system, of sending a note home once or twice a week, can prove very worthwhile. It will also serve to bring the child and the adult—usually it is the mother who will do the tutoring—closer together—and this, too, is beneficial to both. Emphasize to the parent, though, that if any progress is to be made, it will be made only with a positive attitude. If the child is berated, or made to feel he is not achieving quickly enough, more harm than good will result.

While speaking to the mother, you may decide to mention the fact that the child has been a behavior problem. Go on to say that you believe this stems from his learning problem—and that you are very interested in helping him to overcome both. Ask the mother or father to cooperate with you by discussing it with the child, and by showing him that everyone wants to help him. (It is a rare parent who will refuse to do so.) Stress the idea that the child does not need punishment, but he does require assistance, both at home and in school.

You may find many children with similar learning problems or gaps. In this case, we have found the most effective means for coping with this is through grouping.

Grouping Within Your Class

When you discover children who have the same needs, it is a simple matter to form a group, and teach the skills to all of them. You may even if you wish have a bright student teach them—providing you can find a situation where they will subsequently teach the "bright student." Be sure the children realize the groups are temporary—to help them learn what they need to know.

"But," you say, "how can I do this? Not with my class. Hubert screams out, and constantly fights with Stanley. There are several young ladies who are interested in their private affairs. They aren't the least bit cooperative."

1) It is your task to communicate with these children. You must show them that they need to be able to read, and comprehend what they are reading, and this is what you are teaching them. Or they must be able to handle decimals, because our monetary system is based on the decimal system. Whatever you are teaching, you point out, you are teaching because they need it. If you can convince them of the truth of what you are saying, you may gain their cooperation. It is true, of course, that there may be other problems, and we will attempt to show you how to deal with these in subsequent chapters, but we cannot stress too strongly the need for communication with the individual child—and particularly with the one who is the discipline problem.

2) It is important that you never label a child. Take a positive approach, even if he is usually disruptive. When he has had a good day, when he has been cooperative, tell him that same day, "Today it was a pleasure to have you in this class. I know you can

do this type of work every day." The chances are he can—if you gear the work to fit his needs.

3) There are many children who do not have severe learning problems, but who have very short attention spans. These youngsters need a great deal of physical activity. If you do individual or group work with them, vary it. Have them work on the chalk board for a few minutes. Then have them work at their seats. Next talk to them individually. Then structure a class situation, with the entire group participating. The child with the short attention span needs a great deal of variety. Incidentally, this technique will benefit all of the youngsters—for it is an excellent way to prevent boredom. If you realize many of your children have this problem of attention span (and you will find it far worse immediately before a holiday) look for these "changes of pace." You may read something to them aloud. Select a story which is interest-packed, however. And you may have them bring in paragraphs they would like to read to their classmates. Choose, though, material which is attention getting and holding. There are many topics, too, which hold the children's attention. Improving the environment may be one, and even with young boys and girls, the topic will carry the discussion. The child with the short attention span is the one you may wish to send on errands, or have make signs for the classroom. By considering this as a type of learning problem, you can challenge yourself to find a solution for it.

Boys Seem to Learn More Slowly Than Girls

Many people have observed differences in the rate of maturation between girls and boys. We feel that it is because of this that girls are usually the better students, from the time they enter school until college, at which time the boys overtake them. But, in any given class, until then, it is usually the girls who outshine the boys. Their work on concepts, and on comprehension may not differ, but in written work and often in reading, girls' achievements seem to be markedly better. Neatness, too, is a factor which influences teachers, and girls, for the most part, are neater. This maturational difference should be taken into consideration by the teacher. If your boys need more assistance, you may give it to them, or you may arrange groups. Girls can even teach, but, here too, be sure to structure a situation wherein the boys will teach the

girls something. Since boys usually excel in sports, this is relatively
simple to set up.

Our Duty Is to Teach Every Child to Read

We feel that, because of its effect on the future of every child, it
is incumbent upon us to teach every child who cannot do so to
read. This is a tall order, and we realize its implications, but we
feel that it is impossible to overemphasize. Furthermore, far more
often than not, it is the child with whom you are having discipline
problems who cannot read. He is ashamed, he is frustrated, he is
upset—and, moreover, often day after day goes by, and no one is
doing anything to help him to solve his problem. If it is a severe
one, we have suggested he be recommended for special help. If
you are capable, please, please, make efforts in this direction. We
can almost guarantee an improvement in the child's conduct, if
you work with him. We have seen drastic changes in behavior, as
the child's feelings of adequacy increase. We have seen children
spontaneously kiss their teachers, when they find they have been
able to get diplomas upon graduation because their reading has
improved and they have therefore met the requirements. Your
children do appreciate your efforts, your labors, and because they
are getting special attention, they become your friends. Here is
your chance to really accomplish something—to really affect a
change in a person's life. For, more than anything else, if you
teach a child to read, you make further education possible. Without this ability the child is stymied. He can rarely achieve academically—and he is the first to know it. And "The bigger they are, the
harder they fall." The big boys are so often the ones who, when
approached confidentially, will admit, "I can't read." What a
painful admission for any child! If every teacher accepts the challenge, these children will learn. For, where one fails, another may
succeed. But if we duck it, if we hide behind our subject matter, it
is the children who suffer. When they suffer they become disruptive, and then we suffer. The vicious cycle has to be broken.
We suggest, and it cannot be too strongly, that you find out if,
behind all of the calling out, of the shouting, and even of the fighting born of boredom, there isn't a youngster who is unable to
read.

Mental Blocks to Learning

How often have you met a person who tells you, "I have a mental block." One wonders if he really has such a block. He very well may have, for as our knowledge of psychology has increased, we have discovered that procedures which were followed by many teachers were the causes of these mental blocks. To this day one of the authors has suffered the effects of being told, "You are a listener. When the other children sing, you listen." And this in the second grade! Other teachers have called children "stupid," or told them, "This is just too difficult for you." The subject may not have been too difficult, but merely hearing these words from the teacher can cause the child to form the "mental block" of which we are speaking.

You can prevent mental blocks from developing by being patient. If a child seems to be unable to master something which you are trying to teach him, it is best to change subjects, and return to that topic on another day. Perhaps you, yourself, have thought of a different approach. Or perhaps you want to make another try with the previous one, for the fact that the time has changed is important. Perhaps the child is more ready for the topic, now. When you find a youngster who is not responding, rather than hammer away at anything, switch to something else, and return to the problem later. The more techniques you have at your disposal, the better. Ask your colleagues for suggestions, if you find a child resistant to your methods. Ask your supervisor. But do not let the child feel his is the inadequacy. It may remain with him for the rest of his life. And it very often affects his future learning ability.

We know of intelligent people who have never attempted to go to college, because they "knew" they could not pass the intermediate algebra course required for entrance to many colleges. However, we also know of adults who have taken this algebra and done well, after having believed they had mental blocks in regard to arithmetic.

If you encounter a child who probably does not know the term, but who adopts the "mental block" attitude, work with him, making sure he has some success at learning in the subject area, be it reading, mathematics, science or what-have-you. If he feels defeated in his formative years, his learning problems become extremely severe.

Gearing Work to the Children's Level

Discipline problems are far more prevalent when children are not being taught at their level of comprehension. This may be difficult for the new teacher to determine. If the work is too easy, the children lose interest, but far more slowly than if it is over their heads.

Courtesy Official Photograph, Board of Education, City of New York.

Photo 5. Gearing work to children's level.

We know a young teacher who, having difficulty with a group of girls in one of her classes, sought advice from an experienced colleague. He asked her if they ever did their work. "Yes," she replied, "But only when I give them really easy material. So easy it has to be babyish." His sage advice to her was to give them work which appeared to be simple, but progressed, within the assignment, to more difficult concepts. This method works, and works well.

Another means of getting children to try is to begin with games, and bring in the material you are teaching. Everyone seems to love games, and this device cajoles the slow learner. We have out-lined a number of methods which we have found to be effective in our book, *Successful Methods for Teaching the Slow Learner*, pub-lished by Parker Publishing Company, West Nyack, New York. These will help you to work with the child who has learning prob-lems.

We suggest that you begin with work which seems to be readily understood by every child and go on from there. When starting a new topic, determine by questioning how much the children know about it.

"Let's talk about our city," you say. "Who can tell me what services the city gives us? But first, what do we mean by services"? (In this way, you are teaching vocabulary as well as social studies, and are clarifying for the children exactly what it is you are asking of them. Many of them have learned in the first grade about the police and the fire departments. This learning is then enlarged upon.) From the simple services, you would go on to the more complicated ones.

Remember, please, that you must teach the disruptive child (rather than relying on the printed page). It is unfair to gear your lessons entirely to him, and furthermore, it will do little to improve his learning skills, if you do. But you must start at his level, and gradually move upward. Do not be afraid to introduce new vocab-ulary but, please, as you do, make sure that each child under-stands the meaning of the words. Repeat them, have the children use them, and refer to them from time to time. If you do not, they will be lost to all of the children with learning problems.

Give the disruptive child his place in the sun. Allow and, in-deed, encourage him to participate in the class discussions. How-ever, do not permit him to take over the work for, if you do, the rest of the children will become resentful. It is often necessary to take your troubled child aside, to speak with him privately. Do this while the rest of the class is occupied, or after school hours. Try not to use the valuable time of the entire class for any one child. This is one of the mistakes inexperienced teachers often make. They wait for everyone to "get quiet," instead of pro-ceeding with the lesson. If the work is geared to the children's level, if they enjoy doing it, they will become quiet without wast-ing time.

Building the Child's Self-Esteem

The child with learning problems is often the potential dropout, the one whose opinion of himself is so low that he must do something to compensate for it. We have seen such children do many things which are not understandable, except in such terms. They will find reasons to be out of school, since the entire situation is a painful one for them. Often they have forgotten why it was originally painful, but the distaste remains.

From the very first grade, we must make our children feel they can be successful—that even if they are not doing perfect work, it is good, and is acceptable. We must structure our class so that there is an abundance of opportunity for success. How can you do this?

1) By giving simple assignments that every child can accomplish.

2) By gradually making the assignments more advanced, more difficult—and helping each child to complete them. So often teachers give projects and work, and then do not help the child who needs assistance in finishing it. If you give an assignment, help the pupils to complete it. If you do not, some of them never learn how to finish their work.

3) Even the slowest child can do certain things satisfactorily:

a) Make a chart, using drawings, paintings or pictures taken from magazines or newspapers. This is particularly effective in current events.

b) Make montages, using many pictures cut from magazines. Choose a topic, and then have the children look for pictures. Give each child or group a different topic, so that there will not be a run on one particular type of picture. Foods, sports, occupations, means of transportation are but a few.

c) Bring in items of scientific or other interest. Every child can be encouraged to look for such materials.

d) Care for pets, plants or fish tanks.

e) Keep the book or supply closets in order.

f) Make dioramas, three dimensional pictures, models.

Find simple tasks which the child with learning problems is able to accomplish, and you are able to help him a variety of ways, all of which are of significance in building his self-esteem.

It is also an almost undeniable fact that the child who is unable to read well is also unable to write well—that his penmanship, his sentence structure and his use of words are of questionable quality. By assisting him to become more skilled in these areas, you are aiding him in almost every subject area. There are relatively few teachers who teach a child how to write—to physically hold the pen and write, and yet this skill is tremendously important. In order to achieve in school, a child must be able to express himself—in written English. When these areas are neglected, serious deficiencies occur. Any time you spend working with children who need these abilities is an investment in the future education of those children. Your child with learning problems is usually in the forefront of those needing aid in these areas. As he moves upward through school, he must be taught, too, how to study and how to answer essay questions. It is these deficiencies which will help to label him a child with learning problems. Skills, we have found, are often far more an essential part of a child's background than facts. Without these skills, discipline problems are bound to arise.

If a child is over-energetic, and is being disruptive, call him up to your desk, and ask him, "Can you write me a letter, telling me why you are behaving this way? I am really anxious to find out why. I want you to tell me in a letter." The letter will most often be written extremely poorly, and you can then tell your child, "I think you can write much better than this. What do you think? Would you like me to help you to write? I'm sure you realize how important that can be." If the child feels he can write well, show him some of his errors, quietly, politely, warmly but firmly. Get him to see the need that he has to be able to do better written work, and you have taken the first step toward making him improve his behavior. By showing your interest in him, by caring, you start to break down his negative attitude.

CONCLUSION

With every child who is a behavior problem, the first step you take must be to determine the cause. Open the lines of communication—talk to the child—privately, quietly, alone (if possible) but find out what is troubling him. Very often you will discover it is his lack of ability in reading or mathematics. The child, whose lack of skills causes him to become frustrated, and to feel inadequate, is the one who many times becomes the discipline problem in your class—fighting, quarreling, disrupting.

We must try to determine what skills this child is lacking, and teach them to him—or, if a specialist is available, refer him to that person. The gaps in the child's education, however, cannot be ignored, for if they are the problems become worse and worse. We cannot teach this child by having him read an assignment, for the chances of his learning in this way are very small. Other factors should be taken into consideration, too. For example, the child whose attention span is very short, and who needs a great deal of variety in his educational life.

No teacher can deny the need of every child to be able to read and to write, but not every teacher assumes the responsibility for the teaching of these very fundamental skills. Your problem children are so often crying for just such teaching; listen to them, try to help them, and you will find them being far less troublesome in your classes.

The child with learning problems is the one we are duty-bound to help. This is our task—we cannot ask it of parents, or of anyone else. It is the area in which we must really make the most progress, for the child who cannot read or write, or who does not have basic, rudimentary skills, is doomed to failure all his life.

SIX

Working with the Fighter
or the Quarreler

Determining Why the Child Is Fighting

Big or small, fat or thin, boy or girl, bright or slow, when you
have a fighter or a quarreler in your class, you are bound to have
problems. These are the children who cause the incidents and pro-
voke other youngsters to violent behavior. They are the fuse which
smoulders, but which may go off at any time. (Let us define our
terms: usually a fight is a physical altercation—a quarrel is a verbal one.) Yet we do have these children in our schools, and it is incumbent upon us to learn to work with them as well as possible,
and to try to change this pattern of aggression. One of the first
things you must decide is whether a child is dangerous. If from his
behavior you believe he is, we suggest you immediately refer him
to the administration, and to the school guidance staff. Children
who behave in this manner often need the services of professional
counselors, and if a child has been in one fight in your class, discuss the case with the individuals mentioned as soon as possible.
To ignore this incident may mean you are inviting another one. Of
course you will be working with the youngster too, but it often re-

quires a good deal of time before you can obtain any sort of out-side help for him, and time may be of the essence.

Of course there are a myriad of causes and precipitating inci-dents in regard to why children fight. Possibly the most serious is the youngsters have seen it as a way of life at home. They witness disagreements constantly (and, too often, brutality) and, since these usually go unresolved, the child learns a wrong pattern of behavior. If he has seen quarrelling and bickering as a steady diet, one may expect him to regurgitate it in school. Or the youngsters may have anger and hostility within themselves, which has built up over a period of years, and which they give vent to when they are no longer able or willing to control themselves. These emo-tions come to the surface very easily. Some boys and girls are psy-chologically ill, and the compensations and adaptations they have developed may disappear, even temporarily, and break out in fighting. The disturbed children are usually the severest problems.

There are scores of other, less serious reasons. We often live, and go to school, under crowded conditions. Pushing and shoving results, and it doesn't take much for a fight to develop. To prevent this it is incumbent upon us to teach manners, getting along with one another. The population explosion is going to make this a constant problem, for which we should prepare our children.

Attention seeking, very often from members of the opposite sex, is a catalyst. So are deeds such as throwing spit balls, or sticking pins into other people. Tale bearing leads, we have found, to a great many incidents.

These are a small sampling of the precipitating causes of fighting. Our task, however, is not to list them, but to remove them, to take steps to foster friendship and cooperation.

Since we are most interested in avoiding an incident, let us begin with that point.

Stopping Incidents Before They Start

1) At the beginning of the year, or as soon thereafter as possi-ble, establish rules within your class, in regard to behavior. Have the children actually suggest, write on the board, and copy into their notebooks a "Code of Behavior." One of the items should deal with quarreling, another with fighting. Make sure the children are aware of the seriousness of these situations. The time to dis-

cuss them is when there is no heated argument going on, and when the consequences of such deeds can be brought out carefully and clearly.

2) Make the youngsters aware of your expectations—that you know they will use their self control, will respect each other and you, and will be respected in return. Many class discussions of this nature can prove to be very important, and can be a great help in maintaining discipline.

3) When differences between children arise, encourage the youngsters to come to you so that you may act as an arbitrator or mediator. They will do so if they are convinced you are fair and unprejudiced. If you have no "pets," and show no favoritism, they will be inclined to approach you. They feel that you are interested in helping them to solve their problems. We have known of youngsters who have been asked for money by other children and then threatened, but did not go to their teachers with their complaints because they had no confidence in them—and in their ability to handle the situations. You must assure them not once, but several times, that you are willing and anxious to be of assistance, and that you can really help them when the need arises.

Encourage your children to come to you before a fight occurs so that you and they can prevent it. "Johnny is going to beat me up at three o'clock," Mary tells you. You have heard this complaint a score of times. You find Johnny, and talk to him, and to Mary. What started it? More important, how can we settle it? So often you will find tale-bearing, name calling or innocent pushing in the halls to be the cause. Whatever the reason, the most important thing is to settle the argument—to the satisfaction of both parties. Discussion, discussion and more discussion! This is real teaching —teaching the important concepts of life—that we must talk out our difficulties and sometimes make compromises. Is this not the task of every teacher?

4) In addition to the rules in the Code of Behavior, set up rules of your own—as teacher. These cannot be ironclad—leave room for flexibility—for varying them to fit the particular situation. Be firm and fair. Children need rules, and are far more comfortable with them than without them. Knowing that fighting is not tolerated will help to prevent many such incidents—not all, but many. Furthermore, your children will respect you for having established the rules—and for having the strength to enforce them.

5) If there are school regulations in regard to fighting, make the

children aware of them. In many schools, if a child is involved in an altercation, the parents are sent for immediately. If such a rule is not in force in your school, we suggest you establish it in your class. You need the parents' cooperation, in regard to fighting and would send for them anyway. If the boys and girls are aware of this, it usually proves to be a deterrent.

6) In social studies, in language arts, and in every subject area, discuss the importance and the necessity for getting along with others. You are teaching your children to be fine human beings, compassionate, and caring about others. This cannot be a by-product, but it must be a basic concept, taught in many firm, strong lessons. Call it human relations, or brotherhood, or whatever, but teach your youngsters how to work together, and how to try to understand each other. If a fight breaks out, or if children are quarreling, bring these things out into the open by discussing them—attempting to show motivation as well as causes and results.

Teach the positive aspects—the way to talk out a problem, for example. Help your children develop insight into the causes of fighting and quarreling. Give them some ideas in regard to sensitivity—and how easy it is to hurt others. In short, help them to grow into sensitive human beings. Have the children try to develop the habit of viewing the problem from their adversary's point of view by putting themselves in his shoes.

7) Remember, idleness causes activity—often an unwholesome nature. Your children must have a great deal of work to do. Keep them busy on projects of all kinds. Even first graders can work on Picture Dictionaries when they have completed their assigned tasks. Older children can keep library books in their desks, to be read whenever they have finished their work. As soon as a class enters your room, you should have work for them to start—written on either a chart or on the blackboard. This preventive measure is essential for good discipline.

8) Many problems arise immediately before holidays. Children are excited, and anything can erupt, even in the best of classes. You can preclude this if you plan exceptionally interesting work for this time of year. The months after Easter until summer recess fall into this same category. Trips at this time are very worthwhile, and a good way to interest and motivate the children.

9) Never ignore a quarrel or a fight. If you haven't the time at the moment, table it—but do not shrug it off because it may

smoulder and rankle and ultimately break out again. The same is true if a child comes to you, and tells you there is going to be a fight. If need be, keep the youngster with you—but heed all warnings. They may be very important.

10) Never, never leave a class unsupervised. This is structuring the situation for something negative to happen. The times in which we are living are chaotic, and we must guard against this chaos spreading to our classrooms. If you absolutely must leave, place the class president in charge, give the class work to do which they enjoy doing (making up puzzles, writing parodies, writing science fiction, playing written word games) and say, "I expect you to be beautiful people and to behave beautifully. I know you will be." If you have trouble makers, take them with you, or leave them with another teacher.

11) If your potential fighters are hyperactive, give them physical activity to use up as much of the energy as possible. We followed this principle with one child who was a serious discipline problem. He moved 100 chairs from the cafeteria to the gymnasium for an athletic program. This was an excellent means for constructive action. His energies were channeled into useful activity, and he did the job quickly, efficiently, and with much pride. (Let us emphasize again that such activity must be approved by the doctor.)

12) Reward good behavior. So often children are chastized when they're bad, and ignored when they're good. We feel rewards are a most worthwhile technique—such as a picnic or a class visit to the local pizzeria at three p.m. One teacher had a custom—she would take her class, if there had been no adverse incidents, for ice cream every Friday afternoon. Worked beautifully— and her youngsters had been described as "killers." We hope they weren't, but you get the idea. The financial outlay was far less important than the climate in the classroom.

Handling the Problems Which Arise

1) *Without a bell, they're swinging!* What do you do if a fight starts in your classroom?

Use your voice as your weapon. Shriek at the children. Shriek as loudly as you possibly can. Shriek in their ears, if possible. Often this will stop them from hitting each other. It is the least dangerous course of action you can take. Instruct every child nearby to move away, to avoid anyone else getting hurt or involved.

Send two children for help. You should, from the very first day of school, know where to send for help in an emergency situation. Send one child to the principal, to the dean, or even to a strong male teacher in a nearby room. Send the second child to the nearest teacher, asking her to come in, as well.

If your shrieking has not helped, try the following procedure:

Being very careful of your own safety, if you are able to, try to pull the hair of both combatants. This is one emergency measure we have used to separate battling youngsters. However, it may require more than one adult, and you must judge the situation—but be very cautious. A blow in the eye may permanently blind you, and blows to various other parts of the body can be serious, as well. Be sure you grasp the hair of both of the children. If not, you may later be accused of favoritism. If one child is on top of the other, try to pull him off—again, by the hair.

Separate the children. Then help them to calm down—and cool off. Sit them down—but separate them. Talk calmly and quietly with each one alternately. At this point, try to get them to see the problem they have presented—that this is a highly dangerous, most serious situation. It is essential that the parents be sent for.

2) *Determining why the children were fighting or quarreling.* If your handling of these incidents is to prove effective, you must determine why they happen. Here are some questions for you to find answers for:

Have these children been involved in other incidents?

Are these incidents frequent or rare?

Is either child prone to fighting? Does either have a "hot temper"?

Is there a third party, an instigator, involved?

Does one, or the other, of the fighters, have difficulty expressing himself? Often the inability to communicate causes many problems.

Is either of the children mentally slow? Does either have difficulty comprehending the rules?

Is either having problems at home?

Does either child have difficulty relating to other children, to adults?

Does either child have a history of frequent fights in previous classes?

When you have answered these questions, you have clues to handling the situation—with the hope of preventing repeated incidents.

You must first discuss the fight with both parties—as soon as each has cooled off. We have found that discussion is of little or no value when one or both of the participants is still fuming.

In your discussion, bring out the fact that each human being is different, has his own personality, and that we have to learn to take this into consideration. Tempers, for example. There are many people who have "hot tempers," but, you point out to the children, they have had to learn to control them. This control is essential.

If there was a third party involved, what was his or her role? It has been our experience that the vast majority of quarrels and fights are instigated by third parties, who want to see some "action." "So-and-so said you called me such-and-such." or "X said you're going to fight me at three o'clock," or "I heard you said my mother (or father, sister or brother, or even aunt, uncle, or cousin) is a ———."

When there is a third party instigating the difficulty, that person must immediately be called into the discussion. (You may wish to make a rule in regard to this. We suggest, however, that you do this only if the situation has occurred—ex post facto, so to speak. If the children have not been tale-bearing, why give them ideas?) Talk with the instigator and warn him not to continue this behavior. One such pupil can cause an awful lot of trouble.

If a child is fighting because of a misunderstanding, or because he has difficulty communicating a specific idea, it is a relatively simple matter to straighten out. However, the task then becomes a greater one, for this child needs help in communicating and it becomes your work to assist him. Be sure he comprehends why this incident took place, so that he will not repeat it, even inadvertently.

With children who are slow, it is important that the rules be spelled out for them. Incidentally, they very often will interpret your words literally. We told one youngster he could not get into a fight—because of special circumstances in his past history. He did have differences with several boys—and, instead of actually doing battle with them himself, he brought around his *sisters*. He wasn't going to get into any fights, himself!

On Monday, at 8:30 a.m., it is not unusual to hear such words as,

"Mrs. Karlin, can I sit in your office this morning. I know I'm going to get into a fight with someone today." This request is heard not infrequently and I have learned to honor it, because when I have not, the child invariably gets into difficulty—usually within an hour after he has gone to class. Problems arise, but are often unresolved, over the weekends. By Monday, we have children coming in to school who are almost frantic. We shall discuss this situation at great length in a subsequent chapter. Suffice it to say when there is a fight in your class you should try to determine whether either participant was "up tight," or upset—and if so, got into an argument as a result. If this is true, it is usually a simple matter to offer a friendly ear, and allow the child to talk to you privately. Make sure he apologizes immediately, and that the fight or quarrel goes no further. For example, we have seen a boy, on Monday morning, take a poke at a male teacher because he was so angry at his father.

Children who have trouble relating to other children or to adults are more difficult to help. Here, again, your task is to bring the child out of his shell—and teach him to communicate with others. You may need professional help from the guidance staff, as well. But you can assist this child by having him work in committees, with other children. Choose outgoing youngsters who will try to draw him out. Your acceptance of this child will mean much to him. He needs to know you feel he is worthwhile. He is easily hurt, so explain to him you will give him as much attention as you can, but that you are limited by time.

Check into your children's backgrounds during the very first days of the term. Learn which youngsters have had difficulty— and work with each of them privately—telling him you are aware of the problem he has—his temper—and that you would like to help him learn to control it. A temper is an acceptable personality trait, and a child can admit to having one—often, he will tell you, his father has a bad temper, too. Show him how important it is that he learn to control it in school—and encourage him to tell you about his *successful* attempts at control. "I almost got into a fight today, but I held my temper." Encourage him to take pride in this self-discipline.

You will find, too, children who have never fought before, but who become lions. For whatever reason, once a child fights or quarrels, he needs your attention and affection.

Every human being needs this love and affection. Never withdraw it—even when you are angry. This is not to say a child should not know you are displeased. Of course he should—and of course you should and must be displeased. But get over it. Do not harbor a grudge. Once an incident is over, it must be over. Write a report of it for your files, and then let the matter drop. Give the child a second chance—and even a third. By this type of treatment—firm, fair and loving, you teach him to be a worthwhile human being.

Separate fighters. Once children have fought, separate them. Do not allow them to sit together. Often it is the close friends who get into a quarrel or an altercation, and once it is over they are friends again. If they really want to be seated together, and they request this, emphasize the idea that the incident cannot be repeated.

Working with the Class Which Has Fighters and Quarrelers

1) Keep the troubled children as busy as you can. Find work which interests them, and which is relevant to their lives. They often enjoy physical activities—construction, drawing, printing for example. Projects, such as making dioramas, may prove very worthwhile.

Girls, as well as boys, get into fights. This is particularly true in the 7th and 8th grades. We have found, quite often, that these same obstreperous young ladies enjoy crocheting—and it is beautiful to see them working away at their projects.

We have personally told one young lady, "If you get into another fight, you will not be taught to crochet." It actually deterred her from fighting for a period of months. And she crochets magnificently.

2) Have as many periods of physical education as your curriculum will allow. Within these, teach games that require skill—and have the children practice the skills. Use competitions such as races and games to entice the children's interest. Physical education can be the motivation for many lessons, or can be used as rewards.

3) Discuss the concept of fairness. It is unfair to have to spend an inordinate amount of class time on the children who fight, and

the class should be made aware of this. If worthwhile work is going on, and if the work must be made up after school, the rest of the class will pressure the pupils taking up more than their share of class time.

When dealing with any child, stress again this concept of fairness. Make sure that no youngster feels you are picking on him. Assure him, "Whatever I do for you, I would do for every child in this class. If I must be stern with you, I would be with everyone else, too, in similar circumstances."

4) When problems come up, discuss them with the class. Don't hide anything which happens, because children will learn about incidents, and it is far better to have them hear about them from you, than to get whispered half-truths. This technique builds confidence in you, as a person, and you will find children will come to you with their problems because of it.

5) Use the concept of being mature as a basis for discussion, and for your expectations of your children. You may tell them, "I know all of you are mature enough, to discuss this problem." Go into the idea that certain behavior is characteristic of boys and girls at various ages. (We wouldn't tell them, for example, that first graders often pick their noses, but they do.) But praise and building self-esteem is far more successful than recriminations. Tie into this the idea that at their age (whatever it is) they are mature enough to settle differences by talking about them, rather than fighting, and by sometimes being able to accept the advice of other people when they have certain difficulties with which they are having trouble coping.

6) You may wish to introduce the idea that people, whatever age, may be tense, anxious, or in the jargon of the day, "up tight," and that this is the time to be understanding of them, rather than ready to fight with them. We had the experience of having one youngster tell us, after such a discussion, he could now understand why his mother and he fought so often. "There are eleven kids in my family," he told me, "and my father is a seaman. He's out to sea six months at a time—on a tanker." It is possible to do a real service, if you can get through to the boys and girls that their parents have problems, too, many of which the children do not realize, and which can make the adults very difficult to get along with. In this era of the generation gap, any teaching we can do to lessen it is worthwhile.

7) It might be pointed out to the children that if any child is

nasty to them, it may be because the offender is ill, or tired, or has just had problems with someone else. In a word, he may have had a very bad day. And you tell them, "Because we all strive to be worthwhile human beings, we will take his unhappiness into consideration. We will try to be compassionate and understanding, and we will forgive him and let the matter drop." We will also encourage the little offender to go to his teacher, or guidance counselor to invoke the aid of some adult he respects—someone who may help him. Perhaps the older person can, as Shakespeare would say, "Cleanse the stuffed bosom of that perilous stuff which weighs upon the heart."

8) You may wish to allow the children to act out situations in which they express some of the emotions they have, but with which they have difficulty coping. They can compose short playlets, or even act them out spontaneously. This type of activity is more easily done with older children, but you can try it with younger ones, too, giving them more direction. It will probably not work with every class—for you need verbal children, children comfortable with words, and used to speaking, but the attempts can prove to be worthwhile, too.

9) Have the children read stories which bring out ideas of compassion. *To Kill a Mockingbird* is excellent for older children. Check with the librarian (in your school, or in your public library) for others—on the children's level. Whoever can forget Sidney Carton's immortal words, "It is a far, far better thing I do than I have ever done"?

10) It has been found that various activities enable children with problems to work out some of their resentments. A boy banging on drums often can use this as an outlet for his emotions. So can one punching a punching bag. For the more complex, or more talented child, a fine channel for his self-expression is the easel—allowing him to paint freely. The child who has a way with words may wish to write about his problems. In all these ways the children can give vent to their emotions in a wholesome manner.

Gaining Parental Cooperation

It is an absolute must that you and the parents of the children work together—particularly when the child is a fighter or a quarreler. If you are aware of difficulty, it is far better for you to confer with the parents before any overt incident occurs. By speaking with the mother and father, by learning about the child, and by frankly asking for their advice in how to handle him, you may gain information which will be a great help.

In the event that there is a fight or a quarrel, it is usually a school rule that the children's parents be sent for immediately. If there is no such rule, make one for yourself. Parents usually are able to prevent further incidents. They are, for the most part, very cooperative. However, be sure you take the approach, "What can we do, working together, to help your child"? It is most important that you win the parents over to your side. You do this by showing your honest interest in the child, and by really and truly being anxious to help him. We have seen antagonistic parents change completely when they are convinced you are trying to help and teach their child. Many children never fight or really quarrel in all of the years they are in school. Others will have only one or two incidents, largely because of parental disapproval—and parents' annoyance at being called into school under these circumstances. Other boys and girls get into difficulty because of relatively foolish pranks, which can become serious—such as pin-sticking.

Be pleasant when you greet the parent, and say something to the effect, "I am really sorry I had to meet you under these circumstances. Usually Johnny does his work nicely." (Don't misrepresent the facts.) Find something good to say about the child. Then continue with the tale of woe. Finish by asking them to help you to make sure the incident will not recur.

If you are asking them in as a result of your desire to learn about their child, tell them briefly why you are concerned. Sometimes they can account for certain aspects of the child's behavior, which make your task easier.

Do not single one child out. If two have been involved in a fight, you must have both parents in. If not, you can be accused of being unfair, which is devoutly to be avoided.

Even after a fight if you request the parents to come in, be considerate. We suggest a note saying words to the effect,

Dear Mrs. Smith,

I would very much like to see you in regard to John. Would you please telephone me, if 3 p.m. Tuesday, March 31, is not convenient. If I don't hear from you, I will look forward to seeing you then.

If the note is a summons, make it a bit stronger.

Dear Mrs. Smith,

    I must ask you to come in to see me in regard to a problem which has developed concerning Mary. I have set aside Tuesday afternoon, at 3 p.m. to speak to you. I hope this is convenient. If not, please telephone me at _____ to change it. I look forward to seeing you.

Remember, children reflect the attitude of their parents, to a great extent. If the parents are impressed with your interest and sincerity, it cannot help but rub off on the child. And if Billy is a fighter, or Jill carries tales, the parents may be able to stop this behavior—at least in school.

Keeping Anecdotal Records

Because fighting may be, and often is, a symptom of a seriously disturbed child, an anecdotal record should be kept of each of his disruptive activities. This need not be long or involved, but it is a good idea to include the action you take, in response to the child's action. Include, too, the date and location of the incident, i.e.:

March 3
Mary Jane Doe, in a quarrel with Betty Docker, in Room 307. Mary claims Betty pushed her. Betty denied it. We discussed the incident, and Mary was shown the possibility that this was accidental, and that Betty had not meant to push her.

March 31
Mary Jane Doe and Betty Docker in a fight in the girls' locker room. Betty claimed Mary pulled her hair. Mary denies it, says it was done by another child. I saw Mrs. Doe, who told me Mary is quarrelsome at home as well. She said she would try to speak to Mary about this.

April 16
Mary Jane Doe and Bobby Jones fighting in school cafeteria, Bobby said Mary accused him of having taken her dessert from her tray. Bobby denies taking it, said he was just teasing Mary. We discussed teasing, and the fact that every person reacts differently to it. Bobby promised not to do it again. Mary said she didn't believe him.

CONCLUSION

There are many reasons why children quarrel or fight. Some are caused by situations within the classroom, others stem from difficulties at home or among friends. However, our prime interest as teachers is to stop such incidents before they start. We can do this by setting up rules and enforcing them, by making the youngsters aware of the fact that we expect them to exercise self-control, and that we will act as mediators and arbitrators when necessary. Children should be told too, that if they engage in a fight, their parents will be called. This often acts as a strong deterrent. Above all, we must teach them how to settle their differences without fighting, and we must show them how to make compromises.

Because we feel many teachers do not know how to function in the event of a fight in their classroom, we are summarizing below the steps to take. It is possible, indeed probable, you may never need this information, but we believe it is far better to be forearmed. You cannot stand by watching. You must take immediate, firm action. *Steps one, two, four, five and six, are mandatory. Step three is not.*

1) First, you must try to separate the children. You may do this by shrieking—and here it is the sound of your voice which actually does the task.

2) At the same time, you send for help. Send for the supervisor or dean, and also for the nearest teacher. Be sure to prevent any other child from joining the melee.

3) If you feel strong enough, and wish to break up the fight, grasp each child by the hair. However, be very, very careful not to get hurt yourself. The pain inflicted by pulling the child's hair will divert the fight, prevent further injury. (You may wish to find out whether this procedure is acceptable in your school district.)

4) When you get the children apart, send one to another room or to the office—to prevent a recurrence of the altercation.

5) Try to remain as calm as possible, for your own protection, as well as the protection of the children.

6) Never, but never, allow a fight to be ignored. Parents must be seen, and the incident recorded in the children's anecdotal record. The supervisor must be informed, and the dangers of the fight

discussed with the youngsters, privately, and with the entire class.

We personally know of one teenage boy who suffered a brain hemorrhage and died as a result of a classroom fight over a girl. You must know what steps you will take, in advance, and then take them immediately.

However, hopefully, this will never happen, because you will have taken steps to prevent it. By your attitude, by your structuring of the classroom situation, by your awareness of the climate in the room, you can do a great deal to avoid altercations. Even with a child with serious problems in the class, you must help this youngster to cope with them—not satisfactorily 100 percent of the time, but most of the time.

Your most potent method is teaching. Teach your children to try to understand one another, to be aware of problems other youngsters may have. (An excellent composition or guidance lesson is to use the topic "The problems *kids* (use the word) my age have to face." This is usually a learning experience for the teacher, and it can be a tremendously important one.) In using this method, promise the children anonymity. The results may surprise you, even amaze you. You might motivate the lesson by reading letters from one of the syndicated columns of the type which are so popular today. If your children open up, your eyes very well may too.

Teach the skills of making compromises, of being tolerant, and hopefully teach your children, by your personal example, how to love and respect one another.

Remember, too, that parental assistance and involvement is tremendously helpful. Parents should be called in, and informed if their child shows a tendency to fight or to quarrel. Most of the time this behavior is manifested at home as well as in school, but not necessarily.

Where you have children with serious behavior problems, be sure you refer them to the guidance counselor and to the administration. Often such children benefit from counseling, and from the one-to-one relationship. If the counselor cannot help the child to effect changes, he may refer the youngster to an outside agency. The administrators, too, should be made aware of those children who are causing serious difficulty in the classroom—and fighting is surely serious. It is necessary that the teacher, the parents, the guidance counselor and the administrators act as a team, to work with this particular type of problem, for then solution is possible. If the fighting is overlooked, the child becomes more and more belligerent, and the possibility of his functioning in school becomes doubtful.

SEVEN

Fulfilling the Needs of the Attention Seeker and the Hyperactive Child

How many times have you looked at a child and thought, "My goodness, that child just can't sit still"! And you are more correct than you imagined! He almost literally cannot, and expecting him to is almost foolish, for it is a carry-over of the days when children sat with their hands folded, and had to listen—just listen—to the teacher. Unfortunately, this child twitches and turns; he jumps around in his seat; he doodles and draws, or he may fool around, talk and become disruptive. He's hyperactive, has really more energy than he is required to use, and if we do not take this into consideration, we do not meet his needs as an individual.

By the same token, how many times have you thought, "That child will do anything for attention." That, too, is a truism—for in our classes are many children who will, almost literally, do anything for the limelight. Anything may be positive or negative actions—but some action to be noticed.

Attention seeking and hyperactivity are not usually serious problems because neither, as a rule, is born of hostility. They are, however, serious in that they take up an inordinate amount of your time and of your class's time and prevent your children from working and learning. Hyperactive and attention seeking young-

118

sters can cause your nerves to fray, as well as those of their class-mates. Since these behavior patterns have many areas in common, we are considering them together. They are, of course, not the same and we shall differentiate whenever necessary.

Attention seeking is usually the result of psychological causes, whereas hyperactivity is physical. Both types of children may run around a great deal, may jump up and down, leave their seats a countless number of times—to sharpen their pencils, to throw something into the basket.

Both may wave their hands constantly in answer to your questions, and may even call out to be noticed.

However, it is the attention seeker who tries to really dominate the class, who may resort to the use of unsuitable language, and who may dress in an outlandish manner. Neither type of child fits into a mold, nor should we attempt to put him into one. The hyperactive may, as a youngster, doodle, tap or whistle, and this may carry over into adulthood. Sometimes he bites his nails or scratches various parts of his anatomy. He may even be unaware of his actions, until you call them to his attention. Years ago we might have called the child "nervous," a layman's term we rarely hear used today.

Causes of Attention Seeking

The attention-seeking child, we have often found, has many siblings, and may come from a home where he receives little attention (and often little love and affection). In such homes children are to be "seen but not heard." He may act out in class and become disruptive because he knows his teacher will not beat him—although his father might.

However he may be an only child, or come from a small family, but still be starved for attention. Both parents may be employed, and he may be a "latch key child." Or his mother may be occupied with her own interests. For whatever reason, the child has a strong psychological need for attention which is not being fulfilled.

We know of one gentle principal who tells a beautiful story of a pinch on the cheek, and what it taught him. One of the second grade classes was being dismissed, and as the children walked by him, he reached out and very gently pinched the cheek of a gorgeous blond-haired little girl, with baby blue eyes, and red cheeks. The child was truly a picture. As he did this, out of the corner of his eye, he saw one of the little boys nearby stick his tongue out at him. He understood the situation in that instant and went over and patted that youngster on the head, too, for he realized the beauty usually got the attention, and the other child was crying out for it.

There are many incidents of children seeking attention who become frustrated when they do not get it, and do more and more outlandish things. We have seen children come to school in clothing they know is unsuitable, and for which they can be sure they will be reprimanded. Indeed, this concept is very important—namely, negative attention is preferable to none at all. We often recall an incident which occurred when one particular youngster, the son of one of the authors, was three years old. The family was entertaining friends outdoors, and his father was very involved in a discussion—completely ignoring the little boy. When this became intolerable to the child, he picked up a broken branch which had been lying on the lawn, dragged it over, and hit his daddy with it. He knew he would be punished, but any punishment was preferable to being ignored. Very often young children constantly ask their parents, "Why, Daddy"? or "Why, Mommy"? One reason is because in this way they can get and keep the parent's attention.

An attention seeker may be very bright, very slow, or any variation in between. He is usually, though not always, an extrovert, and one movie star we knew personally when she was a child was most obnoxious in the classroom, where she sought the limelight all the time.

Causes of Hyperactivity

As mentioned before, this behavior is generally the result of an excess of physical energy, and a lack of self-control on the part of the child. A hyperactive child need not behave in this manner if he has been taught to channel his energy. Very often he is the child who does not pay attention to the lesson, who does not become really involved in it. We observed one eighth grader literally do a dance while being spoken to by a teacher—and then was most surprised when asked why he was doing it. "I'm not," he replied, most indignantly. "Can't a kid even stand still the way he wants to"?

Effective Techniques to Try with the Hyperactive Child and the Attention-Seeker in Your Class

First and foremost, you must try to communicate with him—to establish rapport, and to get through to him. Listen rather than talk—and try to determine, in your own mind why he behaves this way. Give the child some insight into this, but not too much—do not burden him beyond his years. (We recall one mother, a psychologist, explaining to her four-year old son that he had to return his two year old sister's toys immediately, because the little girl had a very low frustration tolerance. As the words came out of the lady's mouth, she decided to resume her career as soon as she could—that it was unfair to burden her children with such adult thoughts.) Determining the cause of the problem behavior will not always remedy the situation, but will help you to understand the child better.

When the attention seeker or the hyperactive child is disruptive, use the approach, "You are stealing the time of the entire class when you behave in this way, and it isn't fair. I cannot spend a great deal of time on any one child, and it will be necessary for me to ignore you if you continue to behave this way." Ignoring a child can be very effective, but is very, very cruel. While you may threaten to do it, we do not recommend that you do. For these types of children, it is far too strong. Emphasize, instead, the idea of being fair to all of the other boys and girls.

Like every child, the attention seeker and the hyperactive child seek love and affection, and you may find that, sitting quietly with them for a few minutes after school, just talking, can affect their behavior very positively. You are not keeping them in—far from it. Offer them the chance to chat, and see what happens. If you make it compulsory, you are punishing the child, and the entire slant of the interview changes. The children will clam up, and it will take time for you to thaw them out. This is best done on an individual basis, rather than with groups—and is, of course, impossible to do with an entire class. Try to give every child in your class a place in the sun—and a feeling of importance. We realize this is difficult, but well worth the time and effort you make in the direction.

You may be able to sit with individual children while your class is working on compositions, or reading. By doing this occasionally, you can develop rapport more easily. Do not, however, talk to the same children all of the time, for resentments build up. If quiet conversation is necessary, you may be able to use the time when your class is in the assembly, or at lunch, to arrange it.

An extensive research program may help cope with the problems of the attention seeker and the hyperactive child. This involves forming groups, and having each group do research. If the children have not already done this type of activity, you must, of course, give them specific instructions in it. After they have completed the assignments, and it is imperative that you have chosen topics which are of interest to the youngsters, have them report to the class. Make this reporting a formal situation, and invite guests, such as the principal or other supervisors, to make the event even more outstanding. Stress quality, and also the participation of every child, in every group. After such an activity, be sure to praise the work lavishly—if it is praiseworthy. Every child benefits from this, and it is particularly effective with the bright child who seeks attention. The slower child, too, can be successful if you work with him, and if you assign many resources to the hyperactive child, he can be kept busy "looking up things."

Assembly programs are excellent for attention seekers, and hyperactive youngsters, too, and if you can work with another teacher, they are not too difficult to produce. Have the children write their own plays, and perform them. This adds to the value and excitement of the activity. You may wish to set up a Little Theatre, and have groups performing, rather than the entire class. This may supply an outlet for some of the children, attention-seeking and stage-struck, as well. If you find plays which are suitable, and can use an empty classroom, it is possible to decorate it, put up curtains and scenery, and really convert it into a Theatre-in-the round. The children will enjoy doing this, and become very involved. You can then have ushers, stage hands, and a variety of participants. The venture is an interesting, challenging one.

Specific Activities for the Attention-Seeking Child

Class discussions are really enjoyed by the attention seeker. However, it is essential that he does not completely take them over, if they are for the entire class. The town hall approach is good, in which case you may choose him for moderator—on occasion. Panel discussions, too, are excellent devices for giving this type of child an outlet. You may tape record these programs and replay them. Everyone will enjoy this and it serves to motivate the child who wishes to get into the limelight.

Another device you can try is having the attention seeker actually teach the class. When you do this, however, work with the child to prepare him for the task. Show him how you plan a lesson, and how you would suggest he proceed with his. This may be a valuable experience for the child, and we have seen teachers born from such classwork. Here, too, choice of topic is one of the major factors. Allow the child to select his own, and then make sure he researches it thoroughly. Your objective is to make this lesson successful, and any help you can give to the child to accomplish this should be given.

There are attention seekers who will resort to the use of foul language to gain that attention they so desperately need. We feel that, at this point, it is essential that you speak with the child, and make him understand this behavior will not be tolerated by you *because you have very high standards for every boy and girl in your class.* From experience, we know that most children seek to be elevated—and do not wish to be considered in any way inferior. By showing the child that, while he may not be bad, or unintelligent, he gives a very bad impression when he "curses." (Children consider the use of any unsuitable language cursing. We have been told, "My teacher curses." When asked what he said, the child will reply, "Damn it"!) Your emphasis on high standards, you will find, will work. Everyone *wants his school or his home or his work to be the best.* By using this psychology, you can help develop self-pride, which every human being needs. "Not every child can do everything well," you can tell the youngsters, "But you can choose your words carefully, so that they reflect the fine person I know you are."

One wise teacher, when confronted with a cursing problem,

would appeal to the children's pride by saying, "I see that you choose your clothes carefully. You're always beautifully dressed. Why not be just as careful in your choice of words"? She then would continue, "I cannot afford to shop in the same stores as the movie stars, for their prices are far too high. But the words I choose can be just as fine as those of a millionaire. Why shouldn't you? Remember, it costs you nothing—and it makes you just as beautiful."

Try this approach—the results are often surprising. Then try giving the child tasks to do which will make him feel he is a fine person. "Do me a favor, please," you say, "Take this note to the principal's office." Select activities which require the use of language, and make the youngsters aware of your interest in his use of words. It may be necessary to teach self-expression—for many children have very limited vocabularies; this, in and of itself, is most worthwhile. If you can convince your child that he is too fine to be using foul language, you can be of tremendous service to him.

What about the attention seeker who plays the big shot? If we were to analyze him, we would probably find a very insecure person, but we are teachers, not analysts. Here, too, you must talk with this child, and try to get across to him the idea that his behavior will turn people away from him. It is a basic need to want to be liked and respected, and children can understand that, if they self-aggrandize, they will possibly be shunned by their peers. Developing insights of this type may take a long time, but it is time which is very well spent, for the child who plays the big shot is often a disruptive one, who needs attention and private discussion, if you are to reach him at all.

Techniques to Try with Hyperactive Children

First and foremost, the hyperactive child needs much physical activity. He will thrive on health education classes, and if it is possible, you may arrange to have him attend extra classes. (Providing, of course, you get the permission of the other teacher, and providing you work with the child beforehand, explaining why he is being specially programmed, and how he will benefit—but that he must be the most cooperative youngster in the entire class.) You will find running of all varieties is excellent—races, relays, and even jogging. If you have a number of children who require this type of outlet, the establishment of a track team can serve many purposes. The actual performance of the team is not as important, as its motivational value, and the fact that you can have your hyperactive child practicing by running almost daily. Training the child to "keep in shape," and arranging contests will benefit him tremendously.

Courtesy Official Photograph, Board of Education, City of New York.

Photo 6. Giving as much physical activity as possible.

There are many tasks around a school, the performance of which will prove to be beneficial to both the administration and the child. For example, the hyperactive child is a natural for putting up the chairs in the cafeteria, after the room has been used. Bulletin boards need to be decorated, and this is perfect for a hyperactive girl. Most schools use a monitorial staff, and even the counting of notices, or other material which must be distributed seems to satisfy the needs of the hyperactive child. However, it is important that the position never be given immediately after there has been an incident or bad behavior. It goes without saying that the child's doctor's consent must be obtained before the youngster is asked to do any strenuous activity.

As teachers, one of our primary tasks in regard to the hyperactive child, is to teach him how to use his energy constructively. One such young lady of our acquaintance doodles constantly. She reports it enables her to listen more attentively, and she is an excellent student. In our teaching, we should take this into consideration, and when working with the hyperactive child, help him gain insight into ways of utilizing his energy. If the child is lacking in self-control, approach the subject by showing him that he is fortunate, in that he has at his disposal a great gift, but that if he misuses it, he is cheating himself, and others, as well. Suggest ways to him of taking advantage of his physical condition. He may wish to learn to play the drums, or any other musical instrument for example. This would use the energy constructively, and is the most attractive, to many youngsters. Be sure he sees the need for self-control, since this is the key to his life-style.

In certain cases, you may wish to give this child a special series of assignments—such as drawing posters, coloring, taking care of pets, cleaning the classroom, passing the basket around. If you assign these indefinitely, and train the child to do them unobtrusively, not only do you fulfill his needs, but he accomplishes worthwhile tasks, as well.

The Guidance Approach with Both Attention Seekers and Hyperactive Children

Of course you will want to see the parents of either of these types of children. When you do, however, take the approach that you wish to learn more about the child, and that it is for that reason that you are requesting the interview. You may wish to make the point with the parents that the problem presented is serious in that the child is interrupting instruction, and wasting the time of the class. Has he always behaved in this manner? Does he demand attention at home? If he needs more of the parents' attention, can they give it to him? Can the father, for instance, play ball with the child—or tennis—or golf? If there is no father in the family, is it possible for the mother or the guardian to arrange to get the child involved in a club situation, where he can get male attention from the leader? Discuss with the parents the steps you have taken, and seek their cooperation. Do not, however, give the impression you are throwing the whole problem in their laps. As always, your attitude is tremendously important, and you must convey the idea that you are constantly looking for, and trying new approaches to solve the problem. Very often it is a good idea to suggest a physical examination. You may prefer to have the school nurse make this suggestion. However, be very careful you do not frighten or alarm the parents. With hyperactive children, though, it is possible that medication may be prescribed by the physician which will make it far simpler for the child to adjust to the school situation. It is not, however, your task to suggest this. Go no further than suggesting the examination, and do that very gingerly, saying you know how much better Johnny could do if he could settle down. Remember, there are people who will be very threatened by this suggestion. Your lead in may be, "Does Johnny run around a great deal at home? He is full of energy in class, and, unfortunately, sometimes, he is unable to control it. He wastes his time, and I hate to see him do that." Use all of the tact and diplomacy you possess in handling this.

When working with either the attention seeker or the hyperactive child, be sure he understands the fact that, sooner or later, he may lose friends as a result of his behavior. The removal of peer approval, when the child realizes this, may be a powerful means of changing his life style, since this is one of the strongest of social pressures. And very often, the child is totally unaware of this. "Like bad breath, no one tells you," you may tell him. We are not suggesting you implant an anxiety in the child, but that you show him that his shortcomings are very human failings—but, moreover, that they are under his control. After you have established rapport with the child, these insights can actually come from him, if you ask him, "Do you have many friends"? If he says "Yes," then ask, "Real friends"? In most of these cases, if the child is being honest, the answer will usually be "No," and you can proceed from there. If he says, "Yes," then you can ask, "Do you want to keep them"? and follow that line of reasoning. But it is the reasoning which is important, and if you can get the child to see his problem, you have accomplished much.

Because we have discovered, in 1970, teachers assigning such writing as "Write 300 Times I Will Not Talk in Class," we must mention this practice here. Please, don't! It is an anachronism, a relic of the past, and it teaches the child virtually nothing. An assignment of this nature requires no mental effort and will never result in any insight on the part of the child. If you are really exasperated, you may have the child write you a letter, telling you why he is behaving in the manner in which he is, and whether or not he thinks it suitable. You may assign compositions on topics such as "Working Together in This Modern World," and asking your student why this is essential. If you feel the need to keep the child occupied—because you are about to lose your cool, why not have the boy or girl do a poster, decorating it beautifully with the words, "Do unto others as you would have others do unto you."

In each of these activities, which incidentally, may be used under other circumstances, as well, you are teaching something. When you make such an assignment, it is a good idea to give the child some ideas, so that he has a means of getting started. Very often children cannot begin writing, but they can continue, for once started, the thoughts will flow. Or you may have to give the child a whole series of ideas. This is better than having him disrupt your entire class, and again, you are teaching him. Citizenship, cooperation, feeling for one's fellowman—are all so important that we can spend a good deal of time on them, without feeling we are wasting a minute.

We must teach all of our children, but especially the attention seeker and the hyperactive child that they have responsibilities to their classmates, and to their teacher, and that their disrupting causes loss of valuable time. This cannot be repeated too often. We must teach why we have rules and regulations, and that these were made, as are our laws, for the good of everyone. Far too often, your disruptive child feels the rules are for everyone else, and he must be shown this is not true—that the rules and regulations are for the good of everyone.

Above all, in dealing with children with problems, approach them without hostility. This may mean that, after they have been disruptive, you give them something to do, and say, "I will talk to you later, when I am not upset. Right now, I am extremely so." After you have cooled off, you can be far more effective than you could have been at the moment. If you are able to keep your sense of humor, if you can maintain your equilibrium, you are far better able to handle the situation. There are very few teachers in this world, dealing with children, who can be calm and collected all of the time, but if you can avoid dealing with the youngsters when you are angry, if you can laugh when you feel like crying, you come out far ahead.

We watched one young lady dismissing her class. They were

healthy, outgoing seventh graders, and it was obvious that this was a Thank-God-it's-Friday-day. As she managed to escort them out of the building, her face grim, but determined, one of the most hyperactive, a really innocent-appearing boy, came up to her. She looked as if she were about to bite his nose. He was one of her disrupters, and very obviously a "buster." He approached her after the class had left, and we moved closer to hear what he wanted to say to her. These were his exact words, "Good-bye Mrs. Beautiful. See you on Monday." This is typical of the hyperactive child, who, although he causes his teacher much distress and anguish, yet does not feel the slightest animosity toward her. Needless to say, "Mrs. Beautiful" walked out of the building light-hearted and gay.

CONCLUSION

While not really serious problems, the hyperactive child and the attention seeker can take up much of the valuable class time. The causes of their behavior are different but, for the most part, the manifestations are the same. It is essential that you try to develop a rapport with these children, to enable you to work with them. You must also refuse to permit them to waste class time. Foremost in your treatment of these youngsters must be your effort to get these children involved, truly involved, in the work the class is doing.

The user of obscene or foul language usually falls into the category of the attention-getter. By trying to raise his standards, it is possible to effect changes in his behavior. Physical activities are an absolute necessity for the hyperactive child—and your ingenuity in creating these can prove most worthwhile. With both types parent involvement will help you reach, and teach the youngster. Medical assistance may prove to be helpful in certain cases. Remember, these children are rarely hostile, and will react badly to hostility (as most human beings do). They will frequently respond beautifully to a teacher who treats them with love and understanding.

EIGHT

The Underachiever and
the Non-Motivated Child

If you are having disciplinary problems with youngsters in your class who are underachievers or who are not motivated, we feel you must try to solve these problems by considering the youngsters as having learning difficulties, and treating them as such. This type of child is rarely a serious behavior problem. More often he is a nuisance. Since he is not involved in the class work much of the time, his mind wanders; he seeks and finds other distractions. We shall outline techniques for working with these youngsters—aiming toward helping them to improve their learning and turning them away from mischief.

The underachiever and the non-motivated child have many behavior problems in common. Both do relatively poorly in their school work. Both may ultimately become serious problems in the classroom. Both exhibit little interest in the work which is going on, participating as little as they possibly can. Yet there is a very great basic difference; the underachiever, has more academic ability than the non-motivated child. He has shown, as a result of standardized testing, intelligence in reading and the like, that he is capable of doing better work than he is actually doing. He is not living up to his academic potential. The underachiever often has an erratic record. Were you to look at his permanent record card, you would see a pattern which includes high grades on standardized tests (showing his capabilities) and either high or low marks in his regular grades. The reason for this is the variation in demand which his teachers have made on him. If a teacher requires much work, and considers classwork and homework in addition to tests, the underachiever will not do as well as if the teacher gives grades on the basis of tests alone. The reason for this is simple. Underachievers often do well on tests—particularly in their early school years. Their other work reflects the attitude we are concentrating on in this chapter. As the child advances, however, and gets older, his achievement lessens—his marks become poorer— and generally his behavior becomes a problem as well. He is often your spitball thrower, your conversationalist. He's the youngster who looks at you innocently, when you accuse him of wrongdoing, and says, with all the indignation he can muster, "Who me"? He does not consider himself to have problems, but, as far as we are concerned, he does. He can usually be prevented from being a nuisance by a firm teacher. His underachievement, however, needs a great deal to remedy it.

The non-motivated child is one whose performance record on standardized tests, indicates a low-to-middling series of scores. This is accompanied by an equally unimpressive series of grades. The youngster is coasting along. He grasps what he can, but he does not exert himself. He may or may not do his homework, usually does not. He is generally, however, a follower, rather than a leader. If his friend (often the brighter underachiever) says, for example, "Let's go to the zoo today," he agrees with alacrity. (We have a zoo located near our school where truants often spend many hours. It is a favorite place in order to avoid school.) He will engage in mischief because he is bored. He attends school for an excellent reason—there are laws which make it mandatory. But he learns very little. He is not stupid—he has no serious learning difficulties, but his is an untapped reservoir. His mother would probably tell you he isn't really interested in anything special, but he loves to watch television. In class he may annoy you because of his lack of interest, but mostly he is one of the crowd. Much of what will follow will be relevant to both the underachiever and the non-motivated type and, where there are differences, we shall point them out and take them into consideration.

Underachievement and lack of motivation have come to the

fore because one of the major problems facing college educators today is that of the underachiever or non-motivated child who suddenly, when he graduates from high school, decides he wants to go on to higher education. Very often he is simply not prepared, and, even if he is accepted, his days there are generally short-lived. He, and young men and women just like him, account for the sad, sad statistic—that almost 50 percent of freshmen flunk out of college.

The patterns of behavior exhibited by these underachievers and by non-motivated children are often evident in the primary grades. If these attitudes are not taken into consideration at that time, the problems become far more pronounced. It is really necessary that we, as teachers, find ways and means to remedy them as soon as we become aware of their existence. The child's entire future may be at stake. He is constantly being affected. Let us first look at the possible reasons for this behavior.

The Reasons Underachievers and Non-Motivated Students Develop

1) Basically, both of these problems develop as a result of a combination of factors. Being exposed to teachers who will permit these youngsters to do little or no work is an extremely important one. If children have teachers who give them a sense of responsibility, who check their work, who have established standards and refuse to allow a student to fall below these standards, the youngsters develop work habits which preclude their becoming underachievers or non-motivated pupils. If, on the other hand, the teacher is satisfied with a minimum of effort on the part of the pupils, that is exactly the amount of work she will get from them. Far too many teachers fall into this category. Children, even very young ones, are capable of doing beautiful work—if you demand it of them. Some of them will do it, even if it is not demanded, but others, particularly our underachiever and non-motivated child, will get by with the barest of essentials. If the teacher makes a fuss, carefully goes over assignments, discusses the child's work with him, and, when she sees it is below standards contacts the child's parents, the work improves almost as if by magic. If you make this effort, especially at the beginning of the term, the child learns what is expected of him, and, while this learning may need

constant reinforcement, it prevents children from, in the parlance of the day, "goofing off."

2) Another factor which may account for the development of the underachiever or the non-motivated child is the attitude his parents take toward education. If parents are not convinced of its value, their children certainly will not be. In this area you find the interesting situation of the parent who has little formal education of his own, and, to hide his own feelings of inadequacy, gives the child the impression he looks down on "book learning." We personally have encountered such individuals, but fortunately not too many of them. Most parents, if they have been educated, assume their children will be too, and if they have not been, desperately want it for their youngsters. There are also parents who feel free to criticize their children's teachers, and this can have a very deleterious effect on the child. We feel that our conduct of our business, teaching, should be one which is highly professional, almost above reproach.

If we encounter a child who has problems, because of his parents' attitudes, it is necessary that we try to change these attitudes. In other words, we must work through the parents to get to the child. There are so few fields of endeavor in the world today which do not require education, that any parent who scorns it sadly needs educating himself. By carefully discussing this, by showing the parent the effect his attitude has had on the child, by bringing out the need for the training which almost every job requires, perhaps we can affect change in the parent, which will then filter down to the child. In addition to this, it is important that we show the pupil himself what education can do for him.

3) This brings us to a very important third reason. A great many children waste a great deal of time because they, themselves, cannot see the value of schooling. They are unaware of the importance of training, the requirements for skilled and unskilled jobs, and of the position they put themselves into when they do not have the education they need, and cannot compete in the job market. It is our task to teach them these facts of life. Yet this material is found in very few curricula. "Occupations" as a subject area has been mentioned, but has not been widely accepted. It is part of courses in guidance, but surely not required in every school. It is ironic that we can spend hours, as teachers, discussing the wars of the world—but how much more relevant it would be to teach our children how to find their way in the world of work. When you use

this approach with children—that their education is really preparing them for the future, that it is important—sometimes you can convert your underachiever and motivate all of your youngsters.

The youngsters should be able to see immediate value in education. It is difficult for a third grader to look nine years (or more) into his future. How can you show him what he is learning today is important? Find areas which touch his life? Can even young children engage in the battle against pollution? Absolutely! Against litter? Of course! You will find no more willing participants in a neighborhood clean-up campaign. This does not suggest that you announce, "Children, today we are going to clean up our neighborhood," and expect them to rush out to do it. But, with a well-motivated lesson preceding it, they will. A film showing rats, and the connection the number of rats in an area has with the number of uncovered garbage cans and dirt in the streets can motivate the children excellently. A dynamic speaker (possibly the teacher,) a series of newspaper or magazine articles, a filmstrip—all regularly used motivational devices—any of these will give impetus to a neighborhood clean-up campaign.

Check your area for soot. Place a clean, dampened white cloth on your window sills, and have the class examine it. Then investigate—where does this soot come from? Take a walk through your area, looking for litter. One class discovered that, in a large park, there were only two litter baskets. They brought this to the attention of the Park Department and asked permission to construct refuse containers. Of course the request was granted with alacrity.

Relevant education! Important to all children. Especially so to children with problems.

4) Check your underachiever and non-motivated child to determine whether they have specific learning problems. It is possible they have never learned how to study. We have found this is an area far too many teachers ignore. You will find a brief guide at the end of this chapter. Have your children been helped to develop good work habits? Very often they have no idea of how to proceed with an assignment—but their teacher assumes they do.

We have heard of one boy who spoke to a counselor say, "I don't know what that teacher wants."

"But James, you've been in Mrs. X's class for three months."

"I still don't know—so I ain't gonna do it."

"I'm not going to do it," the counselor corrected.

"I'm not going to do it," James replied.

Courtesy Official Photograph, Board of Education, City of New York.

Photo 7. An exhibit prepared by the children to illustrate pollution.

"Can I help you with it"? the counselor asked.

The child looked at him quizzically. "You mean it"?

"Sure," the adult answered, "What did Mrs. X say"?

"She said, 'Write a theme on the Louisiana Purchase.' "

"Why is that so difficult"?

"I don't know what a theme is."

"Why didn't you ask Mrs. X"?

"I didn't want to show all the kids how dumb I was."

It is indeed possible that half the class did not know what the word "theme" meant. Had the teacher gone over the entire concept, and how to do the assignment, her results would surely have been better.

Getting the Underachiever to Achieve, and the Non-Motivated Child to Work

1) Building self confidence.

Both these types of children may become discipline problems if allowed to go their own way, uncorrected by the teacher. The problems develop from the very first grade, and, as is the case with so many problems, the old adage applies,

"An ounce of prevention is worth a pound of cure."

Build up the self-confidence and self-esteem of every child by finding some assignment he can do—and do well. Show him he can succeed, and contribute. Let us return to our environmental topic. Every child can inspect the streets, and can then telephone the Sanitation Department when he discovers an accumulation of rubbish, or whenever necessary.

This is just one of the many ways in which a child can perform a civic duty, and so feel important in discharging that duty.

Bring the reticent child out of his shell. Encourage him to speak. His problems may not manifest themselves as discipline problems, but in time they very well may.

2) Show the underachiever (and the non-motivated child when possible) his academic strengths and develop his interests.

Leonard was a problem in elementary school. His mother was called in frequently by the teacher to discuss his behavior. As he told it her presence was requested, "Once or twice every term." One astute teacher realized this youngster was not being adequately challenged, and, in the eighth grade, assigned a paper on "parthenogenesis." This was the first really fascinating scientific subject the youngster had ever encountered, and it fostered an interest in science which became his vocation and avocation, as well. His behavior improved almost immediately. In high school he became an honor student.

Many youngsters have talents and interests which are never discovered, never revealed to them. We, as a nation, lose a great deal of brain power as a result.

Elevate your children. Introduce them to subjects which may seem, at first thought, to be far above their heads. In whatever subject you teach, find something to intrigue and to enthrall your underachiever and your non-motivated child. This is the first step to changing behavior. Look for the unusual—the out-of-the-ordinary. Many non-motivated children can be captivated by work on prehistoric man. In language arts, science fiction, life on other planets and mysteries seem to capture the imagination.

3) If you have many underachievers and/or non-motivated children, you will find you need extra-special motivation for each lesson. Your introductions, your "gimmicks" are very important

in this regard, for you must entice attention, from the children who are inattentive, and create interest among the disinterested. We saw every child in a 5th grade class come to life when one child brought a dying squirrel into school. The teacher used the situation to great advantage immediately.

"What shall we do"? she asked. "What can we do to keep this little creature alive"? Every child came up to see it.

"What happened to the poor little thing"? she asked the girl who brought it in.

"I found it drowning in the brook," the child answered.

The lesson which followed was a wonderful one—for every child cared. Every child wanted to help. Not just a few—everyone. The story doesn't even have a happy ending because the squirrel was taken to a veterinarian, but he could not save its life. However, the classwork went from animals to drowning, to the value of life. It was memorable—obviously—because the story was told to me by a young adult years later.

4) Teach your underachiever, and your non-motivated child how to study. You may wish to use this short guide. It is addressed to the student.

YOUR STUDY GUIDE

A. To study, one must have notes. Go over the notes your teacher has given you, asking yourself questions about each point. For instance:

What is the importance of this?

Whom does it affect? Why?

How can I remember it?

What connection does it have with what I already know?

B. To study material from a textbook.

1) Read the material and, as you read, make a list of every key word or phrase.

2) After you have finished reading, consult your list of key words.

3) For each word, try to explain its definition or meaning in terms of the chapter.

4) Then, ask yourself to explain what point it is used to make in the chapter.

5) If you do not know, reread the part of the chapter which discusses it.

6) Reread the entire chapter once more.

C. If you are studying arithmetic, select several examples of each type you are studying, and try to work them out. If possible, have someone check your work.

When you find a type you cannot do, get help from your teacher.

D. If you are assigned to write a composition, make a list of your ideas before you start to write. Put down every idea which comes to mind. You may not choose to use them all, but you probably will. You will discover, too, that one thought leads to another.

If you have time, discuss the topic with other people. Their ideas, too, will help you to get more of your own.

Setting Standards

Many underachievers and non-motivated children, as we have said, need to be prodded and encouraged, and need to have standards set for them. We suggest you do the following:

A. Define your assignments very clearly.

1) Because of their problems, underachievers and non-motivated children need clear instructions—including the number of paragraphs, for example, in a composition. While purists might argue this kills the desire to write, we must point out the children require this type of definite assignment to get them to work.

2) If you give an assignment which involves answering questions, have the child copy these into his notebook, leaving space to fill in the answers.

B. Collect the written homework, grade it and return it. You need not grade every word, but if you do at the beginning of the year, you will find it will not be necessary later to grade each paper, because the children develop good work habits.

C. If an assignment is unsatisfactory return it; to be redone. This is most important for the underachiever. Do not accept inferior work. If the child finds he is required to do good work, he will.

D. Discuss his work with him. Make sure he is aware of the requirements—and that he can complete them. If he has difficulty, show him how.

E. Reward children with grades, but only for work done. If an underachiever is given decent grades for little or poor work, why should he try? If he does work, however, his grades should reflect this. Be fair—and show the child the bases on which you are marking. We feel there are children who do not care about getting good grades, but they are in a very small minority. Of these, many feel defeated, and use the "not-care" attitude as a defense mechanism. By showing a child how he can succeed, we can help change this attitude.

F. Have every child keep a notebook, and give him a grade for it. We have found it is the underachiever and the non-motivated child who most often do not do this. They, therefore, have no notes to study from, and no tangible example of their work in school.

Parents will often say, "Doesn't he get any work in school? He never carries books or takes a notebook to school." They are right. If you, the teacher, require, demand and emphasize this, your children will comply. If you are undemanding, you encourage laxity —and the children suffer.

The Bright Child Who Is in Danger of Becoming a Discipline Problem

Let us consider the bright child who is in danger of becoming a discipline problem. Perhaps he does not even fall into the category of underachiever. Perhaps he is doing enough work to get by. But he is becoming a bit of a nuisance, or worse. Is it because his ability is unchallenged, and his imagination untouched? Is he just plain bored?

What can you do about such a situation?

1) Find work which is commensurate with his ability, and which will start him working. Assign topics for him to research and have him share these assignments with the rest of the class. Even in the first grade, the bright child can, for example, tell stories to the children—stories he has heard or seen on television. He can get information from the library—even if someone reads it to him. Older children can be given problems to solve which require obtaining data. They can show films or filmstrips to the class. The child who is scientifically gifted can perform experiments or do demonstrations.

2) You may wish to establish a tutoring relationship in your class between the very bright child and the child who needs help. Fostering a friendship between children of this sort is beneficial to both. The gifted child has an outlet, and the slow child benefits from the help he receives. The teacher must guard against any

show of arrogance or superiority, however. The point to be emphasized is *service.*

3) The bright child can be given a topic to prepare, and told he will teach it to the class. Allow him to do so. This can prove to be very effective as a technique with other children as well.

4) Have the bright but obstreperous child learn to operate equipment such as film projectors, tape recorders, and the like.

5) If the child writes well, he can edit the class newspaper.

These are clues for you to consider as you think of your bright little imp. Individualize his instruction, study him to discover his needs, motivate him, challenge him—and you will probably have little, if any, further difficulty.

CONCLUSION

Should you have underachievers and non-motivated children in your class, it is most important that you do not allow this behavior pattern to continue. For, if a child is not working, he is busy looking for other ways to use his energy. Often these are not significant, except in that they serve as distractions, and as time-wasting devices. These same children can be helped, cajoled, prodded and required to work. If you, the teacher, are willing to make the effort, and it takes a great deal of effort on your part, you can get this youngster to achieve. He will take the path of least resistance, but if you can make him desire to achieve, he will often change his pattern to suit you. We do not mean to imply that you should be cruel or unpleasant, but that you be firm and businesslike. The permissive teacher may teach children many things, and his philosophy is not, by any means, entirely at odds with ours, but we feel there must be a stress on achievement and on pride in workmanship, if the students are to be able to benefit from their education. A child who never takes a note, never reads a book, or never completes an assignment will have a very difficult time throughout his lifetime, for what employer, and what husband or wife could constantly tolerate this? Underachievement and lack of motivation, too, remove from society the contribution of those individuals. And can we, as a nation, afford this?

NINE

The Child with Problems at Home

It takes a very wise child, indeed, to realize how much his behavior at school is influenced by events taking place in his home.
It is impossible for the teacher to be aware of these events unless
the child discusses them and the chances of this happening are not
too great. However, we are all familiar with the stories of adults
"kicking the dog" when they need something on which to take out
their frustrations. How tragically often though, it is when the
"dog" the parent kicks is a child. It is cruel enough when it is a
dog which is kicked—but how much worse when it is a child! This
child then comes to school, and may react in different ways. He
may withdraw into a corner, retreat into himself and attempt to
shelter himself from the world. In this manner he is often ignored.
"Johnny is sleepy today," his teacher may reason. "I wonder how
I can wake him up." But if Johnny is angry and if he does show
this anger by aggressive behavior, he is much more surely noticed.
It is our hope that by our discussion, in this chapter, and throughout the book, you, the teacher, become aware of the varied problems which face many of our children and that you take them into
consideration when you deal with *all* children.

In our capacity as assistant principal, we are in charge of the eighth grade. Discipline cases are brought to us for "handling." A tall boy, whom we shall call Joey, was escorted into our office by two teachers, each holding one of his arms. "He beat up a little boy in his class," they informed me. "We thought he'd kill him. He hit this kid so unmercifully, it was like a nightmare." They removed their restraining hands, but Joey was still shaking with anger.

"That kid laughed at me," he said, "and I had to hit him." He was still so furious it was almost impossible to quiet him down. We telephoned his parents, and spoke with his father, a man of the cloth. "I can't understand that boy," he said. "I just beat him yesterday. He's so stubborn I had to use a cat-o-nine-tails." Upon investigation, the father's story was indeed true, and Joey had the marks to prove it. Is there any wonder that this child had a great deal of anger, and that the first person who crossed him, and whom he could master because of size, he physically attacked. If a child is treated with violence, is there any wonder he becomes violent himself? If he is treated with brutality, how can he help but become brutalized? Joey, subsequently, responded favorably, as is to be expected, to people caring about him. The guidance counselor befriended him, and tried to work with the parent as well. The story does not have a happy ending, though, for the father still, on occasion, beats any of his nine children with that cat-o-nine-tails "because they're stubborn." But Joey has learned to avoid doing things to get his father angry, and so has been able to escape many beatings. This in the 1970's.

Joey's teachers were made aware of the situation, and by understanding, and some loving kindness, helped him to adjust to the school situation. He became aware of his need to take out his anger on his classmates, and learned some self-control. He still got into fights, but less often, and they were of less serious nature than they had been previously.

Problem Areas You May Encounter

The problems we will discuss will be those which affect the child in school—making him a discipline problem. There is a young lady who cannot sit in class—but is constantly asking for a pass, and roaming around the building. When she is questioned, it is discovered her brother is in court—having gotten into some diffi-

culty, as he had on many previous occasions—and the child simply cannot sit still with this on her mind. What can her teacher do?
Talk to her—listen to her problem, commiserate, empathize, understand—and try to help, not with the immediate problem, but
with the child's psychological state *at the moment.*

For a variety of reasons, many children go to school hungry—a
good deal of the time (and are not even aware of it). A glass of
milk is not adequate, and yet it is all many children have, before
they leave for school. In some schools, eating in the halls, and
even in the classrooms is a problem, for numbers of youngsters
who bring their lunches consume them before 10:30 in the morning. (We know of one custodian who has not quite recovered from
the shock of finding pork chop bones in a desk in the rear of a
classroom.) And what of the child whose family does not have adequate income, and who must skimp on food? Surely there are
great numbers of these in certain areas of our country. Or the family on Welfare, whose adult members use food allowances for
other purposes, counting on the children to have "free lunch" in
school. In large numbers of cases, this meal is the only decent
meal the child has during the day. We know of one youngster who
was very indignant when the free lunch program was criticized because, he said, "That's the best I get." But a hungry child often
presents behavior problems. If you have ever dieted, and realized
how cranky you become because of hunger, and the headache
which usually accompanies it, you can realize how the child is
affected. When a boy or girl is troublesome, ask him or her, "What
have you eaten for breakfast"? This is sometimes the key to
solving certain problems. If the child has not eaten, write a note to
the parents, or telephone them, suggesting the youngster eat a better meal. It is one solution well worth trying. If you are aware of
indigents who cannot afford to buy the food, try to arrange for the
child to receive breakfast in the school. Dry cereal and milk is easily managed, and while not completely adequate, far better than
nothing.

There are a tremendous number of separations and divorces in
our country, and their effect on the children of these families is
very great. The youngsters often become insecure, tense and unhappy—and unable to cope with the problem because there is little they can do about it. We have seen fights develop as a result of
an upheaval of this nature, in the background of a child. One very
unhappy child, when assigned a composition on "What I Did

During Easter Vacation," wrote about her parents separating. She actually had had to help her father, whom she loved dearly, move out of the house—and, she felt, out of her life.

When a child misbehaves, it is up to the teacher to try to determine what is causing the misconduct. By sitting down in a quiet place, at a time when both are becalmed after the emotional storm, and talking, it is possible for the teacher to draw out the information. In the telling, the child benefits. Girls, however, are far more communicative than boys, and teachers unaware of this, often feel rebuffed by the young men, who are often far less able to communicate. Then too, boys often see their problems as signs of weakness, and are more anxious to hide them. But by airing problems, children can help themselves.

When you have a child who is normally no trouble, and he or she suddenly acts up—look for a serious problem at home. It is so common to find children taking out their feelings of aggression on their peers—or breaking down because of situations in their lives which they are unable to remedy. The troubled child is often the one who creates problems in the classroom—and if he can be helped, the entire climate in the classroom improves. Encourage your children to confide in you. Help them whenever you can—even if it is only by lending a willing sympathetic ear. Often there is not too much you can do—but listening, and sympathizing is tremendously important to the child.

There are some difficulties, however, with which most teachers cannot cope. Refer these, if possible, to the guidance department, for professional assistance can be very effective in helping troubled children.

The Need for Mutual Trust

Possibly one of the most important aspects of working with children is assuring the child that his story will go no further than your ears. It is amazing just how sensitive boys and girls are in this area. They need the assurance that no one will know of their troubles, or that, if someone else must be consulted, that person be trustworthy. The child should be told of any transfer of information, and asked for his permission before it is released. If he refuses, respect his decision!

We have always told young people we might be consulted if

they had problems, and stressed the confidentiality aspect. A perceptive teacher will see how embarrassed a child can be by not being able to pay his class dues. Problems in connection with sexual areas are very delicate, and need extra-special handling. Often you have to read between the lines, and draw the child out. Many times these can be really serious, complex difficulties.

One can readily see the need for confidentiality when one is asked by a budding young woman, "What can I do to make my father leave me alone"? and you learn that the father is actually sexually molesting *his own daughter.* Yet this is, by no means, a rare situation. It is even more common when there is a step-father in the home. The teacher should realize, though, that confidentiality is as important to the child who asks, "How can I keep my boyfriend—without going too far"?

Confidentiality does not mean, however, that you do not encourage the child to seek help from his parents. Often times talking to them is the very last thing he wishes to do. Yet, if you are able to do so, convincing the youngster to try may be the very thing he needs most to attempt, and sometimes the very thing he wants to do—but for which he cannot find the courage.

When you keep "Confidential Records" they should be just that—for a record open for everyone to read can prove to be an embarrassment to both you and the child.

If a youngster must be referred to another person, do so—but show him why you must make the referral—and that you are not breaking faith with him.

Never tell a parent anything without first discussing it with the youngster, and making sure he understands why you must communicate with his parents. Generally it is a relief to the child—who is often seeking to tell his father or mother himself—but afraid to do so. Also, the child can be sure the family will react better to you—an adult and an outsider—then they would if informed of a problem by their child, alone.

At the same time you are assuring the child of confidentiality, you can discuss the relative universality of problems.

Problems, Problems Everywhere

Is there a person alive who honestly feels he has no problems? Yet to youngsters, these are a constant source of embarrassment—

something to be locked out of the consciousness, if at all possible. But, even if they lock them out, their behavior may be affected.

We have often, in our years as a guidance counselor, told children, "No matter what your problem is—I have heard worse. Not only that, but almost every child I know has problems of one sort or another. Your parents fight? So do they in many other families. You fight with your brothers and sisters? So do they in virtually every family. Don't worry. I guarantee I won't be shocked or surprised—and perhaps I can help you." It worked. The boys and girls "opened up."

The problems children have range far and wide. They may be deeply conscious of poverty—or, at the opposite end of the spectrum, ashamed of affluence. But, by teaching them, privately, and individually, that problems are not to be ashamed of, but are to be solved, you can accomplish a great deal.

Boys small for their age have many problems. Such a boy was Charles. Charles would fight at the drop of an eyelid. He would take on any size boy—or girl; it really did not matter whether he won or lost—as long as he could fight. His astute teacher wondered about it—for here was a child whose baby blue eyes and blonde hair gave him the look of an angel. Yet scarcely a day went by that first week without Charles hitting someone. This while the child was in the third grade.

The teacher, trying to solve his problem, asked, "What can I do with that boy?" Suddenly he realized wherein the difficulty lay. "Charles," he said, "What do they call you at home"?

"Pee Wee."

"And your friends, what do they call you"?

"Pee Wee."

"Do you like it? I'd hate it if I were you."

The child's face lit up. The teacher continued, "When I was your age I was even shorter than you are. I wasn't as strong (Charles squared his shoulders), and I was always called 'Shorty.' I hated it. I squirmed. I got furious. Then I started telling everyone, 'My name is Donald. You can call me Don.' And they did. It was that simple."

"You mean I could say, 'My name is Charles not Pee Wee. But if you want to, you can call me Chuck.' "

"Exactly."

Again—not 100 percent improvement immediately—but 50 percent at least—in this boy's behavior. And by the time he reached the eighth grade, he rarely fought at all! At his request, his name, on his diploma read "Chuck."

Giving the Child a Chance to Express His Feelings Through Language Arts

When a child is suffering from a problem about which he can do little, he becomes frustrated. We are seeing the results of exactly this type of frustration throughout the world. But, if we are to help our children, we must find means for them to express themselves—to vent their emotions. Surely we can do this by talking with them, and most assuredly we should. But often we are totally unaware of problems and really not "tuned in" to them.

We have found language arts work to be extremely effective in this area. For example, we once assigned, as a topic for a composition, "If I Were A Millionaire." We gave this to a class we had been teaching a relatively short time. Many of the works were bright and gay—and some were a bit touching, too—but imagine the impact when we read, "If I Were a Millionaire I'd Buy Parents Who Would Adopt Me and Make Me Feel I Was Their Kid." This came from a seventh grader who became a discipline problem two weeks after he entered junior high school. He lived with foster parents who could not adopt him because his mother was alive and refused to permit his adoption. He refused to accept this, was resentful of them—and was a real discipline problem in class. His behavior was so erratic, so changeable, that no teacher could tell whether he would be civil or impossible on any given day.

Other topics which will help you to learn more about your children are:

1) A character study of myself.

To write on this subject effectively, your class first needs a discussion of what we mean by character—and an enumeration of traits. With this as a basis even a young child can look at himself.

2) How do I get along with my family?
3) The most exciting thing that ever happened to me.
4) My hero, and why I think so.
5) Happiness is. . . .

We actually had a child tell us that happiness was having his own room. His family, receiving public assistance, had been moved to a larger apartment. The only boy in a family of seven girls, he craved peace and quiet. Who are we to be surprised?

6) My best friend—and why I like him.

7) If I had three wishes, I would ask for. . . .

8) How can *I* improve *my* environment?

9) How can I bring more happiness to my family?

10) What "love" means to me.

11) If I were Alice in Wonderland, I would. . . .

12) Can modern medicine ever defeat death?

13) How can we stamp out hunger?

14) A trip into the future.

If you use these topics, do not read aloud any child's work to the class, without permission. Indeed, tell them, in advance, that this composition is a communication between them and you.

Incidentally, in grading this work, give it two marks. One for content, the other for written English. Can you imagine how our boy, asking to buy parents would have reacted to a grade of "C?"

Composing Playlets for Self-Expression

There are forms of psychotherapy which utilize the playlet technique, for it does supply an excellent vehicle for expressing oneself. It is, for instance, particularly valuable to draw out the very quiet child—the one who generally comes from a big family—and is almost begging for attention. It gives him a chance to be seen and heard.

To use this technique, begin with a discussion of the situation. Set the stage somewhat this way saying, "There are many problems which people have—lots and lots of people. Let's act one out. We can start with a scene at the dinner table. The family is just getting ready to eat."

Next choose children to play the roles. If you have youngsters who are particular discipline problems, select one or two of them.

Have the children compose the dialogue as they go along (à la Fellini). Encourage the children to really express themselves—to really throw themselves into the play. Help them to "let themselves go" in the various parts. When the subject has been exhausted, discuss the playlet. Did it make any particular point? Was it of interest to the audience? How might it be improved?

By this method, you are able to show the universality of problems, a concept which is always of great value.

Family problems are well-handled by this technique, as are those arising from puberty and developmental changes.

We recall one playlet with delight. It was structured around lateness—and getting out of the house in the morning on time. From this, it moved to the use of the bathroom—eight people and one bathroom to be specific. The "family" sat around and talked about their problems. One of the children suggested they draw up a time schedule. Others objected, but since no one could suggest any other *feasible* possibility they decided to try it. (Remodeling the house to include a new bathroom was suggested but the "children" realizing their "father and mother" could not afford this, vetoed it immediately.)

In addition to the solution of the problem, the playlet also became addressed to selfishness, and to considering the rights of others. It was time exceedingly well spent, with realizations of these concepts brought home to the children.

Assuring the Child He Is Judged by His Behavior, Not That of Others

What effect does a "skeleton in the closet" have on a child? So often children are extremely sensitive about problems within their families—over which they have little or no control. If it is possible for you to assure the child that he is responsible for his own behavior, but only for his own behavior, you can help him immeasurably.

Areas of sensitivity are many and varied. How does a child feel when he knows the local newspaper carries a story, "Jonathan Green arrested for armed robbery"? Particularly when other youngsters say, "That's your brother, isn't it"? How is this child to react? Surely the teacher is tactful enough to avoid mentioning the article, but invariably other children have seen it. This is the time for a class discussion centering around the topic, "Each person should be judged for his own behavior." You may wish to bring into the discussion Edwin Booth, the famous actor, and John Wilkes Booth, his infamous brother. In this situation, consider and discuss the *class* as if it were a family group. By your warmth and sincerity you can influence your children. If you believe what you are saying, so will they.

The troubled child needs special help from you, at this time. He may, understandably, be upset. Taking him to lunch and talking with him can work well. By showing him you care, that you are interested, and that you would help if you could, you offer him a boost which may not be forthcoming anywhere else.

But, what about the child for whom it is more difficult to feel sorry—because he behaves as if his brother is a hero? He adopts the manner of a braggart, and swaggers around in reflected glory. It is essential that you speak to him, too, and if possible, get past that attitude, for, if no one does so, this child may imitate his "hero," thereby getting into trouble himself. By indicating to him you are sure he is a worthwhile human being, who will be able to make his way in the world without resorting to breaking the law, you may be able to be a deciding influence on his life. Making him feel important, in the class situation, may accomplish wonders in this direction. Perhaps you can figure out tasks for him to do, such as caring for the fish, or changing the bulletin board displays for you, being a monitor, or collecting milk money. Whatever it is, if he can feel some thrill of accomplishment, it will work in the direction of making him a "big shot" in an acceptable sense.

Participation in team sports can be very effective in giving a child a positive self-image, and can change a youngster's behavior pattern—in some cases almost as if by magic. We watched this happen in the case of one young man we shall call Lester. Lester was thirteen years old, the fifth oldest in a family of eight boys. He showed signs of following in his family's footsteps, but at a rate unbelievable for one so young. Two of his brothers had already been convicted of armed robbery. Lester was tall for his age, and pleasant looking. He said very little. In the movies he would have been labeled the "strong, silent type." It was difficult to get to know this boy.

Lester was absent the day of the basketball tryouts. His homeroom teacher discussed the boy with the coach and it was agreed the child be given a chance anyway. He did beautifully; seemed, indeed to be a "natural." Before he was accepted for the team however, the coach told him the rules, and reinforced the idea that if Lester was involved in any activity which was even suspicious in nature, he would be dropped immediately from the team. The boy gave his word—and he kept it. From his first day as a player, he was a different youngster. His is a real success story, for he went on to play high school, and then college and professional basketball. His interest in, and love of, the sport had enabled him to overcome his home environment. His brothers never did.

Just as an excellence in sports can help a child to grow and develop well, so can an interest in music. Many famous musicians have overcome handicaps through this interest, some of these handicaps having been environmental, others physical or psychological. The point, of course, is that a child needs to feel he is a worthwhile human being. We must help him to feel this way.

If you become aware of a child having difficulties at home, judge carefully before you mention them. You will find many children are very upset—and even the mention of the problem can break them up. If you feel you should bring the subject up, do so, but with the greatest tact of which you are capable. If the child wishes to discuss it further, do so by all means. If he seems reluctant or reticent, do not pursue it. The wound may be too raw.

The death of a parent is a most traumatic event in the life of any child. You may be surprised to find the child's prime concern is, "Who will take care of me?" Children realize their dependence on their parents—and when one is suddenly gone, their insecurity may be extremely serious. Some are willing and even eager to talk about the loss—others not so. This wound is one which takes a long time to heal. (One wonders if it ever really does.) We have seen children burst into tears—at the slightest provocation—after such a loss.

James, a thirteen-year-old, had been a very disruptive child. He told teachers off, in no uncertain terms, whenever he had the desire to do so, and in language which made him unique in the entire school. If an adult touched him, he became furious. "My father will get you," he would say. "My father will come up to this school, and beat the hell out of you. You just wait." In due time his mother was called in to see the principal. Her first statement was "James hasn't been the same since his father died two years ago." A check of the record revealed the truth of her words. James had never been a problem until the fifth grade. Right after his father's death, in an automobile accident, he had suddenly become upset almost as soon as anyone spoke to him. The anger he felt at his loss manifested itself in this way. He was sent for psychotherapy which, in time, helped to improve his behavior.

Explaining the Changes in Customs and Mores

Customs and mores have changed so quickly in the last five years that an entirely new system of standards (or according to your thinking—the lack of them) has been established. It is difficult for us, as teachers, to affect the thinking of the parents. However, if we are able to reach the children, we should do so with the basic idea in mind that they become aware of the changes and try to present them to their parents in a manner which will be acceptable to the adult mind. "Things sure aren't the way they used to be," parents will say. And, indeed, they certainly are not. The days of children being seen and not heard is over. We approve of this, and firmly believe children should have some say in determining their lives—but we are against it being an entire say.

If we can inculcate and reinforce feelings of respect for parents in our classroom, these will come through when children and parents are having discussions and differences at home. If a boy speaks with respect to his father, his long hair and blue jeans may become more acceptable to his dad. It is often the means young people use which alienates their parents, as much if not more than the end. It is worth your time and effort to work toward mutual respect from a moral standpoint, of course; but also from a practical one. A child who has been fighting at home will fight in school. More important, a youngster who has no positive feelings toward his parents will rarely have them toward his teacher.

Bring out with your youngsters the reasons for the existence of many customs. If they've outlived their usefulness, say so, but stress the need for keeping an open mind.

There are, however, situations where parents must make rules and enforce them. If you can show your youngsters why this is true, you can cause really important learning to take place. If a child learns, for instance, that most young people have curfews, he is less likely to object to them. There is little we can do to stop a parent from hitting his child, but if the child can accept the fact that others have curfews, too, and can go along, obeying the rules, he has been helped. The same is true of doing chores. If many young people do them, the individual will not feel put upon.

Changes in ways of doing things do not have to be overnight to be effective. But youth is in a hurry—and because of this, problems in the family often arise. Discussions of these problems with an unbiased adult often prove to be very valuable for, while youngsters often will not listen to their parents, they will to their teachers! "Why can't I smoke"? the twelve-year-old asks. If told by his parents, "You will probably become a heavy smoker," he gets furious. You say the same thing, and it is differently accepted.

Giving Added Attention to the Child Who Needs It

Shakespeare called it "The milk of human kindness." Surely called by any name, compassion is a beautiful emotion. Children with problems at home need it—desperately—and often have no one to turn to. Whether you teach a child for the entire school day or just for a small part of it, you can help him. How? By calling him aside, at some time during the day, when you have a few minutes, and saying very quietly, "I know there is something bothering you. Is there any way in which I can help you"? If the child doesn't respond, you may wish to add, "If you'd like to talk to me about it, I'm glad to listen. Can you come to my room at lunchtime (or at three—or whenever)"? Once the appointment is set up, let the subject drop.

Don't be surprised if the child "forgets" the appointment. Very often he will, if the subject is painful. But, if he needs to talk, or is receptive, he will approach you. Should he do so, listen to what he tells you. Sometimes there are things you can do to help. At other times, all you can do is listen. Referrals, for example, would only be made with the child's permission.

When there is a language problem, very often you can help. People who do not speak English may experience many difficulties in the course of their daily lives. We know of more than one teacher who arranged for financial assistance—once for the widow of an Army man, killed in action!

Remember, there are problems which are tremendously serious to a child, but not to an adult. Never, but never, laugh at a youngster confiding in you. We have seen one girl completely broken up at the death of her turtle. Mere mention of a replacement brought more tears! Peculiarly, what comforted the little girl were the words, "We all have to die sometime."

"Gee," she said, "I never thought of it that way"!

Children with strongly autocratic parents are often terrified of them. Mary Elizabeth, a little blonde, told her teacher, tearfully, "I just can't go home with this report card. My father will beat me." It's possible. Parental brutality is far from unknown in our society. One young man has run away from home four times as a result of excessive strictness on the part of his father. His mother is completely dominated by this man, as are his other children. Only our young friend has tried to escape.

Child suicides, too, are a possibility to be considered. If a child makes a threat of this nature, don't take a chance ignoring it. He or she may never take any such action, but you cannot judge this yourself. Discuss the remark with a guidance counselor or with your principal, and with the child's parents, as well. We were discussing this subject with an experienced teacher. "Never, in all my 18 years, have I had this happen," he said. "I don't know how I would react." About a year later he ran into our office, saying, "I'm so glad we had that talk about child suicides. I'm really upset—but I can imagine how I would be if we hadn't talked about it." There are many reasons a child may make this threat—but none negates the seriousness of it.

In our typical "happy homes" there are often serious clashes of personalities, which engender terrible conflicts in the minds of children. There are overly-strict parents, and overly-permissive ones. The latter situation is of interest because these children, placed in a normal school situation may not be able to cope with school or class rules and regulations. There are parents who drink, others who are drug-oriented. What goes through a child's mind whose mother often behaves peculiarly when he returns from school because she is intoxicated?

In every case, when a child misbehaves, try to learn about the situation at home. This knowledge can often help you to comprehend the child's behavior. Give those children who need it extra attention before they become discipline problems.

I once asked a girl, whom we shall call Jeanne, where a friend of hers lived. I knew the address, but not how to get there.

"Why"? Jeanne asked.

"I would like to visit her mother. She told me her mother is too sick to come to school."

"Please don't," Jeanne warned. "If you do, she'll be so ashamed.

"But, why"? I pursued the discussion.

"They're poor," Jeanne answered.

"But she is always dressed so nicely," I responded.

"But, Mrs. Karlin, they really are so poor they only have beds. There's no other furniture except a table and chairs in the kitchen."

How right Jeanne was! The humiliation for her friend would have been dreadful, because in school, this child always looked her best—but at what price?

If a child misbehaves, listen to him—with an open mind and an open heart. Perhaps you can help to ease his burdens. At least you can learn what "makes him tick."

CONCLUSION

The influence of family and home life on the behavior of a child is, without question, undeniable. There is no doubt that children are tremendously affected by events in their personal lives. We must always consider the possibility of this when a youngster, who previously has been self-controlled and cooperative, becomes disruptive. Our first action should be to seek the cause of the change of behavioral pattern. There is always the chance that it may be something which is happening to the boy or girl in school but, more frequently, it will be rooted in events occurring at home. By listening to the child, by getting him to talk to us if he is reticent, by sympathizing, by doing everything we can to help him, we can often make it possible for him to function in the classroom. We must, above all, show him that we are truly interested in him— that we really care.

Confidences must never be treated lightly, nor allowed to become gossip over the luncheon table. How devastating to hear a teacher say to her friends, "Do you know who's getting a divorce? The Does! Would you believe it? Mary Jane told me about it today"! We are certain no self-respecting person could reveal anything of this nature—unless she was not aware of what she was doing, and was not thinking. A child's secrets are indeed precious. Accepting them implies you have assumed the responsibility of not revealing them.

Often children are comforted, we have found, when they discover they are not the only ones with problems. It is almost strange, but when there are others "in the same boat," some of them are helped to cope with their situations. Yet they rarely talk to other boys or girls about their difficulties until they reach the teens. Helping children to bring their difficulties into the open is another way in which we can help them. Often they need to give vent to some of their frustration, and this can be done through the written word, as part of the language arts program. If a topic which allows them to do this is presented to the entire class, it can prove helpful to any child with a troubled mind. Spontaneous playlets are another technique which is useful in this area. We must assure our children, too, that they are judged by their own behavior, not that of others. This is important if a sibling or parent is involved in legal difficulties.

We are living during a time when the so-called "generation gap" has become a household word. There was always a gap, but it seems to be infinitely wider now. If we can help to bridge this gap, we can provide assistance to both parents and children, thereby making their lives a little happier. The child with a problem at home will often cause a problem in school. By your treatment of him, as a human being, you can help to erase some of the effects of this problem, thereby helping him to learn and exercise self-control in your classroom.

TEN

The School Phobic, the Truant and the Loner

Perhaps the most bewildering situation a teacher can encounter is that of a child who is a school phobic (literally one with a phobia which is focused on school attendance). Despite the efforts of the teacher, and he may make a great effort, this child resists coming to class. Like the truant, the phobic is a deeply troubled child, but for different reasons. His pattern of behavior is often the result of an overprotective mother. For reasons of her own, her interests are served by having her child with her. We have seen mothers who would encourage their children to stay home, who would write excuse notes for imaginary illnesses, and who would go so far as to hide the child when the attendance teacher visited the house. An interesting aspect of this problem is this—often, when the child reaches twelve or thirteen, he finds himself inadequate in his school work and then refuses to go to school. His mother, now being prodded by the attendance authorities, tries to get him to come to school. Terrible scenes may ensue, or quiet ones; we have often seen both—when the child will not enter a classroom. This overprotection by the mother is one cause of school phobia. There are many other reasons, of course.

Another is the youngster who has been conditioned to dislike school because of unhappy experiences—with teachers or with children. One lady of our acquaintance was considered by many to be a superior teacher—and, indeed, for almost every child in her class she was. But she would choose one youngster to scapegoat—and make that child's life miserable. A close friend of ours still gets red-faced and upset when he talks about her—and he was a student of hers (and a scapegoat) 32 years ago! Children may be traumatized by being called "stupid," or by any unthinking, insensitive remark from a teacher or another adult—or from a child. Remarks, incidentally, of which the person saying them may be totally unaware.

Truants are youngsters who do not come to school—here, too, for a variety of reasons. Often they feel tremendously inadequate and consequently inferior to the other children. Billy was such a boy. He was polite and handsome, and could verbally express himself without difficulty. In the sixth grade he became a truant. He had never learned to read, and now, in the sixth grade, he was older than the other youngsters, and his self-respect was at stake. He found two boys willing to find outside interests, and rarely came to school.

This brings to mind the influence of other children. The opinions of peers are very important to most boys and girls, and when a child finds friends who are willing to "play hookey," he is really tempted. If he has had negativistic experiences as a result of truancy, he will not become a truant; but if his parents ignore it, or if they do not show him their disfavor strongly, he may develop this type of behavior pattern. If school holds little interest for him, or if he is not motivated to learn, the influence of a truant friend may be very effective—and very detrimental.

The loner really is quite different from the school phobic and the truant. This is a child who has difficulty establishing relationships with others—adults (teachers) or children. He or she has not learned to talk to others, or to feel comfortable with them, and, as a result stays by himself or herself. The loner will often bury himself in books or hide in corners, not because he doesn't like people (although he very well may not), but because he is shy to the point of it affecting his functioning. And because the child is alone and lonely, he may develop into a school phobic or a truant. It is for this reason that we will consider him in this chapter.

Perhaps the outstanding case of a child who was a school phobic, but who started out being a loner, was Leslie. In an era when one could tell at a glance whether one was talking to a boy or a girl, one would have to stop and figure it out because Leslie looked more like a boy than a girl. Her hair was short, she wore boy's shirts, *with* ties (which she knotted perfectly) and her walk and talk were more masculine than feminine. She did not care to associate with girls, had never played with girls' toys, and was the neighborhood "Tomboy." But her manner was so unpleasant that boys as well as girls rejected her. She was sarcastic to a point where no remark she made could be accepted at face value.

She was the oldest child in the family, and—you've guessed it— her parents had wanted a boy. Even the name they chose for her was often associated with the opposite sex.

Leslie refused to come to school because she felt no one liked her—and the children made fun of her. She had friends outside of school, she told her teacher, but they were older. She tried to go to class, would get to the door, and turn and run away. She sat in the guidance counselor's office for hours, days, weeks—refusing always to enter the room. The counselor worked with her, arranged for a child, a girl, to act as her "buddy." About two weeks after this situation was set up, the "buddy" came down to see the counselor. She said, "Leslie invited me to her house, after school. There were a lot of tough, older girls there. No boys. Just girls. Leslie is very friendly with her landlady. I didn't feel comfortable. Do I have to go if she asks me again? I don't want to hurt her feelings."

Leslie has previously been referred for psychiatric help—and, when this story was told to the counselor, she telephoned the social worker in charge of the case. Upon further study, it was discovered Leslie, at the age of thirteen was a practicing lesbian. It was necessary to remove her from school and from her home before any effective help could be gotten for her. But it was her refusal to go into class which brought the matter to a head, and which initiated the psychiatric help the child needed so desperately.

This is, of course, an extreme case, because most school phobics are certainly not homosexuals. However, school phobics do have serious problems, as do truants, for, if they are not helped, their futures are at stake. The prognosis is poor. Both need expert help —both in and out of the classroom. Referrals for professional therapy should be made. There are, however, a number of things which a teacher can do to help the situation, and it is to these that we shall address ourselves. However, it usually is the professional help—by attendance personnel and by psychotherapists, working with parents, which will get the child into school. The teacher must take it from there.

Attendance personnel are trained to work with children's problems of this nature. They communicate with the student, himself, and with the parents. Whenever possible, they offer concrete assistance. We have seen the attendance teacher work wonders—not with all children, but with some. They sometimes spend hours and hours talking with individual children and their mothers or fathers. They seek out the parents, often visiting the child's home to do so.

Communicating—Really Communicating with These Children

If you can develop rapport with the school phobic, the truant or the loner in your class, you can help him—but if you do not, he will come and go, scarcely touched by his encounter with you. Developing rapport takes time and effort, but it is a must if you are to succeed with children with these problems. If you are able to get the child to discuss his life style with you, you may be able to determine the reasons for his behavior. It is difficult for a child to admit he has no friends or that he feels tremendously inadequate. The other youngsters may tease him, and make his life miserable. If, on the other hand, the teacher becomes his advocate, the spirit of helping the child will become infectious, and it is hoped, and often achieved, that some of the other children may develop a friendly feeling for him.

One develops rapport by talking and by listening. Ask the child if he can tell you why he doesn't come to school. It may be possible for you to help directly—as, for example, when a child in the class is annoying him. The old archenemy—poverty—may be depriving him of a pair of shoes. Try to find out what, specifically, the problem is—and if you can help him to solve it.

What else can you, the teacher, do to help the loner, the truant or the phobic?

Create a pleasant atmosphere in your classroom. Many children will seek to avoid a teacher who screams at them. They may develop all sorts of fears, and often fantasies, as a result of being the scapegoat of the teacher or of other children in the class. The peer group, too, can be a tremendous factor in making a child feel comfortable or uncomfortable in school. It is your task to create an accepting relationship among the children—and most important, that you, too, show the child you accept him. You accept him—problems and all and you really care about him. If you are able to do this, your work will be a source of deep satisfaction, both to the child and to you.

1) When the child is absent, you can have a talk with the rest of the class. You can tell them you know they are compassionate, kind and anxious to help each other. "And here," you say, "is one of your classmates who is lonely and not particularly happy, and who needs companionship and attention." You should say you are sure the children in your class will help by extending themselves, by offering him friendship, and because they are friendly people, they will listen to his problems and try to help him. Should you try this method, we feel you will be pleasantly surprised by the cooperation the children will give you. Mention, too, that in helping the child, they are helping you. Indeed, this is a favor—a big favor—they can do for you.

2) Enlist the help of the officers of the class—asking them privately to be friendly to these children who need friendship so desperately. Approach, too, those children, who have shown a sympathetic nature.

3) Seat the children with problems near warm, outgoing youngsters—with whom it is easy to make friends.

4) Have the class do committee work, causing interaction among all of the students. Find out what talents the problem children have—and structure the situation so they can use them—be they drawing, painting, musical, athletic or literary.

5) Discuss the children's problems and obtain the cooperation of other members of the staff—so that the principal, assistant principal and the other teachers will have a kind word and smile for them. This helps to make school a pleasant place to which the children will want to come. By sending the child on errands, and what child does not love to run errands, he feels important and he has the opportunity to speak with other teachers.

6) Praise the work these children do, whenever you can, and display it to call attention to their talents and abilities—even if it is so simple a thing as doing a hand spring. Sincere interest, a pat on the back, a smile, a kind word—these are the antidotes for truancy and its pernicious side effects. Warmth and affection are the

penicillin which we can use—and we can use it lavishly and effectively.

7) In any manner you can think of, nurture the child's self-esteem. Let us do all we can to make him less unsure of himself. It has been said each person makes his own price tag—so it behooves us to enrich the child's belief in himself.

8) The problem child might be given a specific set of chores which he is responsible for, and which he knows are essential to classroom management. This nourishes his self-importance, and, in a pleasureable way, develops his sense of responsibility. He may take attendance, or distribute the milk, collect homework or clean and wash the blackboards. These tasks, because of their importance, make the child feel needed. Here, too, is an opportunity for the teacher to awaken a social sense in the children.

Inform the parents, so that the child's mother is able to say to him, "Your teacher is depending on you to (and she names the task). How can you stay home and disappoint her?" Discuss this with the parent beforehand—and recommend she use the approach just mentioned.

The Parents, and Their Reaction to the Problems

In all of these cases parental cooperation cannot be over-emphasized. Be extremely careful you do not antagonize the parents —handle the situation with the utmost delicacy, tact and understanding. The parents, too, may feel threatened by you—and it is essential you eliminate their fears by your attitude and your understanding. Invite them—rather than summoning them—to see you. Your interview can be done very effectively over a cup of coffee, or even over lunch.

When a parent is summoned, she comes in worried, anxious and often upset. The kind teacher senses this and makes every effort to put the parent at ease. He states at the very outset that the problem is not a monumental one—and that, with the cooperation of the parent, is often soluble.

Begin your interview with an affirmative statement. Find something praiseworthy about the child, and say it immediately. This will help to ease the tension the parent is probably feeling. Then state the problem succinctly—neither over nor underemphasizing it. Next, ask the parent for his suggestions. How can the problem be remedied? In the case of phobics, truants and loners, the parent must be made to realize how important his role is—and that he must be firm and steadfast in his insistence upon the child's going to school. The habits the child develops now will become part of his adult life. A sense of responsibility must be developed as early as possible in the child's life—if he is to ultimately become a happy, useful citizen.

In the case of truants, phobics and loners, special counseling may be necessary—and the parent should be encouraged to accept it. The seriousness of non-attendance should be brought out —lest the child form unwholesome and undesirable associations. Truants often become involved in robberies, and other serious misdemeanors, and are ready victims for drug peddlers.

Many parents face up to reality with extreme reluctance. It is the duty of our teachers and supervisors to help the parents to face up to their problems, and so the possibility of solving them can be achieved.

It is dangerous, indeed, in this day and age, to stick our heads into the proverbial sand. Better a little action now than tragedy later. Children who are not in school often get into serious difficulties. These are the truisms the conscientious teacher or administrator will emphasize to the parent.

Ollaf was a bright, mischievous youngster whose behavior was extremely erratic. He was capable of doing good work in school, but often did not bother to do so. He loved to "fool around." One day the child was sent for by the principal, who had received complaints that a child fitting Ollaf's description had been seen overturning garbage pails in the neighborhood. One landlord had threatened to let his dog go after the boy if it happened again. Ollaf was not in school, but this was not unusual because he often took days off at a time. The principal telephoned the parent, asked her to come in to talk with him about Ollaf. She was very resistant. "I know he's full of the devil," she said. "Why do you have to see me"?

The principal insisted. "Please come in on Monday, anyway. I feel I must talk with you."

The conference was never held. The mother called to say she had guests from out-of-town, and would be "too busy." Another appointment was set up, and that one was broken, too.

One month later the principal attended Ollaf's funeral. He had again engaged in over-turning garbage pails, and the landlord had done what he had threatened to do. He had turned his dog loose, and Ollaf, to escape from the animal, had run away—right in front of a truck. The principal had tried to convince the parent that there was a serious problem, but the mother had totally resisted his suggestions, and even his admonitions that "Something had to be done."

It is also mandatory that the teacher notify the parents whenever absences occur for serious accidents may be precluded in this manner. Far too often children "play hookey" and parents are unaware of it. This is unfair to both the offender and the parent. Preferably telephone calls, or post cards or letters are simple, effective devices for this notification.

Parents must be made to realize the importance of attendance— in order for their children to obtain an adequate education. How unfair it is for a parent to keep a child home to babysit or perform chores! This deprives the child of his heritage—his schooling. In this case it is the parent who plays a key role in habituating the child to attend school regularly.

Try to have the parent leave every interview in a good frame of mind. If you are sincere, she will feel you are trying to help her and her child, and her cooperation is well nigh insured—to the best of her ability. However, parents, in these cases, are often unable to do very much with their children. Do not expect miracles —and do the best you can. Be sympathetic as well as firm. It is to be hoped that the child can be helped by both parent and teacher.

It might be wise to enlist the aid of the father. However, in a great many cases, he is absent from the home, and it is his very absence, and the inability of the mother to cope with the child's behavior which has caused the problem to arise. In this case, if possible, it is wise to notify the father, and to enlist his cooperation. If the father is absent from the child's life, perhaps a counselor or a male teacher, or even an older brother can substitute and be helpful.

We might suggest the parents reward good behavior. They might make a party if a child whose attendance has been poor shows a marked improvement—or give him other rewards.

The teacher might be asked to notify the parents when the record shows this improvement. Accenting the positive, rather than the negative, is a very effective way of building desirable habits.

Studying the Records for Relevant Information

Very often a thorough study of a child's record will reveal a great deal of pertinent, valuable information. It is possible to see a behavior pattern developing. A youngster has been on record as having attended school regularly. Suddenly he changes? Why? Often this change will coincide with family problems. Has the parents' marriage broken up? Has the mother had to go to work? Is there now inadequate supervision of the child? Does the father drink to excess? Is there enough money to meet the needs of the family?

Are there problems with other siblings? The death of a parent can cause tremendous psychological effects. Even the passing of a grandparent can have strong emotional repercussions. When you discover the cause of a child's problem, you are far better able to understand and work with him. However, be very careful of the manner in which you approach him, for he may be very sensitive about his personal life—children very often are.

He may have a physical problem. Is he a stutterer? Are his eyes in good condition? Has his hearing been tested? Is the child small for his age? Is he possibly a victim of malnutrition? Or, to the contrary, is he overweight—a compulsive eater, for instance. A check of his records might disclose also, a psychological or emotional problem. If you are aware of this, you can be a far more effective teacher—for the same reason a physician can be most effective when he has a clear picture of the cause of the malady.

Very often psychological problems manifest themselves as physical ailments. Ulcers are classic, in this area. The overweight child may be a compulsive eater. A skillful teacher might solve this problem of overeating by unearthing some talent the youngster might have, nurturing it and giving it full expression. It is entirely reasonable to suppose that the child might substitute pursual of this talent instead of spending many hours eating.

We must be extremely knowledgeable of every child's idiosyncracy. For instance, one boy of our acquaintance cannot be screamed at, and if he is, he becomes violent, shrieks back, flails his arms—and causes a free-for-all in the classroom. We found it necessary to advise each teacher never to raise her voice when speaking to this child—regardless of what he does. He must be spoken to quietly. This is the only effective way of reaching him. Gentle words work like a charm upon this particular child.

There are children who are very frequently ill—and who are classed as constitutional inadequates. Their absences are usually legitimate and they should be given every consideration insofar as making up their schoolwork is concerned. I have in mind a little girl whose extreme pallor and frail body bespeak her inability to face the hardy routine of daily work. The perceptive teacher, by observing such a child carefully, will realize that here it is the staff, and not the rod which is needed. Like every other troubled child, she required tender loving care—physically and emotionally as well. Her record disclosed this irregular pattern of attendance all of her school life. This, of course, is easily understandable.

Making the child feel comfortable, and the problem less important.

When a child's attendance is erratic—because of phobias or truancy, or when he is a loner, he particularly needs to be made to feel he is part of a group, and at ease with them, and with his teacher.

1) A youngster should never feel afraid to come to school. We know of one case where a little boy was being blackmailed by an older child, who attended a nearby high school, but caught our little boy en route.

Another little boy reported he is unhappy at school because, if he talks or even squirms, his teacher writes his name on the board, and leaves it there for the entire day. This embarrasses him—but he says he cannot help squirming, and often, involuntarily, he will say something to his neighbor in the course of a long school day.

If you have a child with excessive absences, ask him, not in a derogatory tone at all, but in a sympathetic, inquiring voice, "Dear, is there someone or something bothering you in school, that makes it hard for you to come to school"? Such words as these may be the "open sesame" to the child's life style at school or at home.

2) Help him achieve success in some area. It is not absolutely essential for this child to achieve proficiencies in every subject as it is to discover his forte, and to encourage and help him to develop it. This will make him happy as well as useful in school.

3) Give him an on-going project to work on—one that he likes, and that will supply a reason for coming to school. Can you use music to induce him to come to school? Teaching him to play the harmonica, the recorder or the guitar might do it. Make this a

year-project, with frequent musical interludes. Or if there is a child in the class who can play an instrument, could he teach others? Could he produce an assembly program?

Find a project, really involve the child, encourage its development—and he'll come to school.

4) Effeminate boys often need a male "model." If you review their histories you will often find there is no older male in the family. A gym teacher, for instance, can help such a child to achieve normalcy. It is essential that this problem be dealt with with all delicacy, lest the child become an object of ridicule.

5) "Let's start fresh."

At the beginning of each term, make sure each child feels he begins with a clean slate. Past misdemeanors should be forgotten—and everyone has the opportunity to begin anew. No teacher should ever come to a classroom with preexisting ideas. (The word *prejudice* is born of the word *pre-judge.*) If a child has been an attendance problem, or a problem in any other way, make no mention of it. Here silence is indeed golden. However, if the problem does become manifest in your classroom, it is well to point out to the child privately that, in the light of his past record, this is a specific weakness of his which you, as the teacher, would like to help eradicate.

CONCLUSION

The school phobic, the truant and the loner are considered in this chapter. These are the children who, for one reason or another, do not come to school. Getting them to attend is usually the task of the school administrators, but it is the teacher who must work to keep them coming. What can the teacher do? He can attempt to communicate with the youngster, to establish rapport, and to determine what the problem actually is. Why would the youngster rather stay away? The teacher can try to structure the classroom situation so that the child feels comfortable and welcome. If possible, the cooperation of the other youngsters in the class should be requested. Activities to give the child with problems some measure of success should be created by the teacher. The troubled child should be given responsibilities within the classroom—so that there is always a reason for him to attend.

The parents' aid must be enlisted—and, if need be, the parents should be educated in regard to insisting the child come to school. The child's previous records should be studied for clues. How can the teacher best reach this child? The boy or girl should be questioned, kindly and gently to determine whether he is having difficulty because of a situation within the school.

The teacher must constantly behave in a positive fashion toward these children when they do come to school. They need much sympathy and compassion. It is easy for a teacher to become annoyed when a child, with whom he has been working, rebuffs him by staying out again, but one must treat this philosophically. One must be a benevolent diagnostician. What is making this child stay away? What powerful drives are acting upon him to cause his absence? What entices him elsewhere? If he believes the teacher has a sympathetic feeling, he may disclose his secrets. Does the child feel "out of it"? Is his personality recognized in the classroom? Are his good works on display?

A word, a touch on the arm every day when the child enters the room, a smile, a little private discussion—in other words, some small token of recognition—may be the magic which will bring the truant, the phobic or the loner into school—perhaps even regularly.

ELEVEN

The Physically Handicapped Child and the Child of Poverty

Determining Whether the Condition Has Seriously Psychologically Handicapped the Child

We are considering the physically handicapped child and the child of poverty in the same chapter because there are many similarities, and many methods will apply to both types of children. Physically handicapped children are those who are in some manner restricted because of their physical condition—be it poor hearing or eyesight, the loss of a limb, malformations or malfunctions of any part of the body—or children whose size produces feelings of inferiority.

The child so handicapped may have psychological problems resulting from his inability to perform at the same level as his peers. If he feels different, this may cause him to be frustrated and angry, and may result in his being a problem in the classroom. Let us report one such case. We saw one little boy throw himself down and bang his head against the floor—in sheer fury. He was in the first grade, and his mother had truthfully told his teacher the youngster had temper tantrums. "He doesn't listen to me," she complained.

169

The teacher, after the first episode of such behavior, spoke to the child. He watched her intently, gazing at her with beautiful eyes wide open. She sent him back to his desk, then called to him. He ignored her. She called again. He still paid no attention. She tapped him on the shoulder, and he whirled around. This young woman suddenly was struck by an idea, "My God," she thought, "he doesn't hear me." And that, of course, was the problem. The child had lost 75 percent of his hearing, yet no one had spotted this loss until she did. This story has a happy ending—for with a hearing aid, the child's frustration disappeared. It would be wonderful if we could work such magic all the time—unfortunately we cannot.

The child of poverty may feel just as frustrated as this child with the hearing loss. He may live in a slum or in a slightly better community—but if he is poor, the results of this poverty on his psychological development may have caused him to have many problems. Ours has been called "the affluent society," and for many people it is. However, living in the midst of plenty, but not sharing in the cornucopia of riches, can cause hurts which warp the personality almost beyond belief. We, as teachers, cannot ignore this, cannot close our eyes to the problems of the child of poverty in our classes. An example: We saw a supervisor reprimand a child for wearing improper dress. The girl had on a pair of shorts, which she was reminded she knew was against the school rules and regulations. The child agreed it was, and she knew it. She took the verbal lashing without a word of reply, then burst into tears. "My sister took my skirt, and I tore my dress," she said. "This was the only thing I had to wear." The supervisor was really upset—because the girl's story was, without doubt, the truth. Yet this woman is a compassionate person—but, unthinkingly she had wounded this little girl—whose psyche could not withstand such onslaughts.

In working with a troubled child, we always seek to determine the problem. In the cases mentioned, we must try to determine whether the physical handicap or the poverty has done psychological damage. One good method is to have the entire class write a paragraph on the topic, "If I Had My Way I Would. . . ." Careful reading of the papers may give you insight into the troubled child's mind. Surely talking with the child will help—both him and you. He will benefit from your understanding, and you will benefit by learning to know him better.

You may teach a class with many poor children. If you think about it, you will find that some have been far more badly scarred, psychologically, than others. It is often the case that the deeper the scar, the more difficulty you will have in selling the child on the idea of self-control. There is no question but that the conditions in the entire world today reflect, in part, these deep psychological wounds.

Poverty has insidious effects as well as obvious ones. If a pregnant woman eats a diet deficient in vitamins, particularly Vitamin B, scientists believe the intelligence of her unborn child will be diminished. However, most children do not utilize all of the intellectual potential that they possess, and can achieve far more if we, as teachers, structure the situation so they are motivated to learn and to achieve.

If you are teaching in the lower grades, in a disadvantaged area, make it your most important goal that every child in your class must be able to read. In a word, that you will furnish for each and every child, the key to all knowledge—for reading is indeed, this precious key. If this becomes your personal goal, you will be amazed at the permanent effects you can have on the lives of your children. In the upper grades, should you discover a child who has not mastered the mechanics of reading, it behooves you to even start from the very beginning, if necessary—if this child is to acquire anything resembling an education. One highly successful teacher, who retired after 40 years of teaching, was asked, "Did you ever have, in your entire career, any children you couldn't teach to read"? She thought for awhile, then answered rather shamefacedly, "Yes, two." Yet she had taught in a very poor area —which is still poor, but which now has, unfortunately, many, many children who cannot read. Her goal had always been, "Every child must be able to read when he or she leaves my class."

Finding All Possible Assistance for Either the Physically or the Poverty-Handicapped Child

Communication is the first step to be taken if the child is to be helped.

1) We shall always remember the little boy who said to us, one morning, "Teacher, please excuse me for being absent yesterday. My Mommy and I sat up all night because we were afraid the rats

might bite the baby." This incident occurred many years ago. Unfortunately, it could still happen today. While we have seen improvement in housing conditions, there is still a very long way to go.

2) Every child should be encouraged to discuss his problems with his teacher, or with someone else in the school who is interested in helping him. How can a teacher foster this? One way is by quietly talking privately with the youngster, and asking him questions. If need be, every effort should be made to obtain help from appropriate social service agencies. In most schools the guidance department may be able to give some advice to families in need of financial assistance. For those deprived children who come to school without breakfast, make every effort to see to it that the youngster gets it in school. Lunch is doubly important, too, for the child who has not eaten is very likely to become irritable, and may become a discipline problem as a result. And, of course, it goes without saying that malnutrition will affect his development physically and mentally and spiritually. If you have any inkling of a child's need for financial or other help, be sure to refer him to the guidance counselor, or to the principal or one of the supervisors. The astute teacher will make the referral to the adult that he thinks is most sensitive to the children's needs. It is of paramount importance that the child be made to understand that this measure is in no way a disciplinary one—that the intent of the referral is to help him.

Sometimes the P.T.A. Organizations have been known to "pitch in" to assist in matters of this kind. They have supplied clothing and shoes for example for children who have not been able to come to school because they did not have adequate protection from the elements.

Assistance for the physically handicapped child depends first of all upon the discovery of the existing defect in the child. Certain defects are very obvious—a withered arm, or lameness, for instance. Others, such as a heart condition, poor eye-sight or poor hearing are disclosed by a review of the health record cards, and also by regular physical checkups.

We recall a very trying experience we had as a young teacher. A little girl in the class refused to take her medication, and would pass out into a state of unconsciousness. This caused considerable disruption in the classroom. This child finally had to be excluded from our regular class, and placed in a special group for handicapped children.

If you have physically handicapped children, the wisest thing to do is to discuss the children with the school nurse, the school doctor, and the parents as soon as possible. Confer with the guidance department as well. Speak to the previous teachers and when the children are promoted, be sure their conditions are noted on the record cards. It would be worthwhile to talk to the new teacher about their ailments—they will be grateful to you for having done so.

Let us always bear in mind that whatever physical activity or exercises these children take part in must be done with the complete written consent of their physicians.

Helping the Child to Function in the Classroom (If Possible, Before He Becomes a Problem)

1) Sit down, as early in the term as you can, and try to communicate with the child, showing him that you understand his problem—be it physical or economic—and that you feel for him, and will help him as much as possible.

2) If he appears to be frustrated, help him to get rid of some of his frustration. If he can handle them, give him physical activities which utilize some of his pent-up emotions. Health education can be very worthwhile—for it is far better for a child to hit a baseball than to hit another child. It is interesting to note that the children of poverty have become renowned baseball players, for their emotions have been channeled in the proper direction. The city streets and sandlots provided the early baseball diamonds.

3) If the child is in an angry mood, if he realizes he can, with impunity, speak of his frustration to his teacher or supervisor, disciplinary problems can sometimes be avoided. A little boy once approached his teacher and said angrily, "I'm gonna punch Jackie in the nose. He laughed at my pants." Indeed, the trousers were torn in an embarrassing spot. The teacher said to the child, "No, darling, don't do that. Go into the gym and hit the punching bag as much as you like. Then come back and we'll talk about it." This may seem to be unorthodox, but with a child who is so pent up, the best way to handle the situation may be by first giving him a

physical outlet, and then, when he has calmed down, discuss the problem. (It includes talking with Jackie, too.)

4) Youngsters have, at times, been quite cruel, and laughing at a physically handicapped or poorly dressed child is far from unheard of. Staring at him is often more insidious. It takes a great deal of work with a group of children to get them to understand the pain the child who is handicapped may feel—as a result of the unthinking behavior of others. This is a very important aspect of our teaching—to help all of our children to become sensitive to the feelings of others. You can, of course, see how necessary it may be—if you have a child in your class who is the object of such behavior.

5) If a child is not achieving academically because of his frustration, with his life or his physical handicap, this adds to his problems. By helping him to keep up with his classmates we at least eliminate an extra source of frustration. If he is learning, he feels satisfaction as a result of this, and is more comfortable in his mind as well as in the classroom. Academic failure often results in rejection of the teacher, and of the material he is teaching.

6) The child with sight or hearing deficiencies, for example, must receive special consideration. Consider Lloyd, a boy who wore thick glasses, and who made a constant nuisance of himself —in the back of the room. His teacher was an inexperienced young man, who did not perceive any problem—other than the fact that Lloyd was a behavior problem. It was the librarian who suggested to the teacher that perhaps the boy could not see from the back of the room. "Don't ask him," she said. "Let's ask the school nurse." Upon investigation, it was found that Lloyd could not possibly have seen the board from where he had been seated. As a general rule, *any child who has either a visual or a hearing problem should be seated at the front of the room.* It is worthwhile to check to see, too, that no child is seated behind another child taller than he is so that his view is blocked. This simple measure may prevent problems from developing.

Supplying Physical Needs Through Social Service Agencies

The liaison person dealing with social service agencies in most schools is the guidance counselor, for one of his professional duties is to be aware of the services available in the community.

There are various types of organizations offering many types of assistance. Confer with the counselor when you have a child in need of help. The assistance may be financial, or it may be that offered to handicapped persons. In either event, a consultation with the counselor may prove exceedingly worthwhile. Funds for eyeglasses, for instance, were obtained from the American Red Cross, for those children unable to pay for them.

When a child misbehaves a great deal, you can win him over by talking with him and by showing a sincere interest in him. What is a better manifestation of this interest than helping him to find solutions for his problems. When children know you are sincere in your desire to help them, they respond to you as a person. We have actually heard one youngster verbalize this, as he said to his friends, "Let's be good for Mr. X," as they entered the classroom. And they were right, for this teacher really "gave a damn" about the children.

Teachers are often the first English-speaking people with whom immigrants, not speaking the language, come into contact. If we can help them with their problems, we influence their entire thinking about our country. Here, too, your liaison is through the guidance counselor.

There is money available from the federal government for establishing work programs, such as the Neighborhood Youth Corps. You may wish to bring this to the attention of the principal. With this program, individual children may be recommended for jobs. This should not be announced to an entire class, however, for there are not that many positions available.

We recently met a young man on his way to church. He said he had been working for the summer, because his mother had been ill, and he was trying to pay her doctor bills. He had gone everywhere seeking employment, and had finally been sent to the Neighborhood Youth Corps. He was dressed beautifully, but inexpensively, and his manner was that of a serious young gentleman. It was very difficult to believe this was the same boy who had been suspended from school because he would not stay in class but insisted upon spending his time in the halls, the lavatories and the nearby park. But now, with an actual problem and the opportunity to solve it, he was really rising to the occasion. How fortunate there was a Neighborhood Youth Corps—for he is only fourteen. It was this organization which enabled the child to help his mother, and foster his own sense of responsibility.

Raising Self-Esteem

We believe, and much research has been done bearing this out, that children can be encouraged to achieve, and their self-esteem raised, when they are made to feel they are capable human beings. You may wish to try this method: Tell your children, if they are in the fifth grade, or above, "I have asked for all of you to be in my class." They may look skeptical. Some may be children with problems. Indicate your awareness of this, saying, "I know all of you aren't perfect—but who is? This is a heterogeneous class. Of course you don't know the definition of that word—but *hetero* means different, and *geneous* means grouping. It is a way of saying each of you is on a different level of learning. I plan to experiment with you—to make this the best class on this grade."

This technique does work. If the children still are skeptical, add, "Is there anyone who is not willing to take part in this experiment"? Ask for a show of hands. Usually children do want to participate in experiments. Explain then that you will keep records—and also inform them of exactly how the experiment is progressing. Build on this—by using diagnostic or pre-testing, and following the lesson with achievement tests (of your own—not the standardized variety). Construct the tests so that your children do well—everyone of them.

When a child is handicapped—it is essential that he do well. Spend more time with him, if he requires additional attention. Have other youngsters work with him. Build on the idea of an esprit-de-corps, of the achievement of the entire class. With everyone working together, you teach one of the truly important lessons of life—cooperation.

Children who are handicapped by physical ailments or poverty very often feel defeated early in their lives. You can, by structuring situations carefully, negate some of these feelings. It is most important that you do so.

With younger children, do the same thing—but omit the discussion of heterogeneity if they cannot handle it. Children, told they are the best class, and convinced of it, will behave that way—but do not tell them this if it is not believable.

Making These Children Feel as Important as the Others

Children with problems are often conditioned to defeat. It seems to be all they expect of life. Their experiences in school seem to emphasize this, and their feelings of unimportance grow and grow. How can we change this? How can we make them feel as important as the others? One of the best tools you have at your disposal for this is the establishment of positions as monitors, as outlined in Chapter One.

Make your youngsters, who need to be made to feel important, monitors of the highest order. They may, for example, greet guests, or serve as guides during the occasions when parents visit the school. Prepare sashes of the school colors for them to wear, and ask them, confidentially, if they can wear white shirts or blouses, for the particular occasion. If you can arrange for them to be in the color guard, on assembly days, this, too, is a great honor.

You may choose such children to write on the board, serving as your "right hand." (Or your left, if you happen to be a lefty.) However, do this only if the child's writing is easily legible. To allow him to serve in this capacity, if it is not, is surely not doing him a favor.

Seat the children with problems near you. The proximity to the teacher, with a few confidences from you, will do wonders to make Johnny or Susie feel "like a big shot."

When a child is physically handicapped, try to help him to do every activity the other youngsters can do (providing you have his doctor's permission). Allow him to play baseball, for example. This can do a great deal for the child, toward making him feel equal to the other children.

Taking Trips to Broaden Horizons

Children handicapped physically or by poverty need to have their horizons broadened, for far too often their parents have been unable to travel with them. When we use this word, we mean going *anywhere* for we have met children who have *never* (never) been more than one mile from their homes. This is true for many reasons—the two most common being lack of funds and lack of initiative. It is as much a part of our professional work to introduce this aspect of learning as it is to introduce any other.

To facilitate taking trips, use small groups. Divide the class into units of five or six children. Place any discipline problems in different groups. Choose (or have the youngsters choose) a group leader for the day and that child becomes responsible then, for the others in the group.

Before any trip, prepare the children for it by discussing why you are taking the trip (what you expect the children to get from it), and give an assignment to be handed in afterwards. Also discuss with each child who is a problem what you expect of him in the way of self-control. Singled out, in a one-to-one relationship, you should be able to convey to the child your sense of urgency that the trip be a good one—and that he show he is mature enough to handle it.

We very strongly believe that no child in a class should be prohibited from taking a trip. The children with problems are often the ones who need the experience most. However, be sure the children understand their responsibilities. Lack of funds should not prevent children from participating. You may either have each child contribute a bit more to cover the expenses of the others, or you may seek aid from the Parent-Teachers' Association, or from school funds.

Trips are an excellent opportunity to meet parents. Use it when you have a child who is presenting problems. Invite his mother to accompany you on the trip, and spend some time talking with her. Learn about the family, about the youngster's earlier childhood. Communicate your difficulties. By always using the concept, "What can we do, working together, to help your child"? you may be able to obtain the aid of the parent—which very often makes a tremendous difference in the behavior of the child.

Setting Up Projects

Project Work: Much can be done by project work to raise the children's self-esteem. The troubled children, we have found, react extremely well to a large project situation. Decide with the class what type of project they would like. It might be a travel fair, with children working in groups of twos for each country, or for each state. (You might wish to work with sections of the country.) Perhaps your group would like to set up a bank, to show the many services banks offer. For science classes, an exhibit showing the various branches of science, biology, chemistry, physics, geology, anthropology, psychology, then the specialties, botany, zoology, physiology, etc. Consider a class project on occupations—methods of transportation or means of communication. Try a dissection of a newspaper—with each committee showing how articles are constructed.

However, to use such a project most effectively, have it displayed, and invite the parents, the principal, and other important people to see it. Also, motivate the class. Make sure participating is a privilege, and then help your troubled youngsters. Give them advice and material. But help them to do projects which they, and you, can be proud of. You may be forced to have a discussion privately with your troubled child, "I know you would like to be part of this project—wouldn't you? Have I your word you will cooperate? Is there any help I can give you?"

Be sure, that if you divide the class into groups, the troubled child is placed with youngsters who will continue to work—and will not be led by him. Try to find children who will exert favorable influences on his behavior.

Be sure all work is labeled with children's names—so that the youngster, himself, sees his accomplishments—and so that visitors, too, see them.

CONCLUSION

Ours is the richest country in the world. Ours, then is the power to eradicate poverty from every nook and corner of our land. We have gone a long way in defeating poverty, but we still have much further to go. We know very well how economic misery destroys the physical, mental and spiritual well-being of our children. The child of poverty is ill-fed and ill-dressed. This has a marked psychological effect on him. Should he become a discipline problem in class, it is absolutely essential that we try to understand him and that we try to help him to solve his problems.

The same feelings of inferiority are, too frequently, true of the child who is physically handicapped, and he, too, desperately needs the compassionate teacher, whose gentle words and sympathetic manner toward him can do much to build his self-esteem and his self-confidence. By being cognizant of the child's talents and abilities, and by giving him every opportunity to display them, this child can be made to feel as important as any other child in his class. If the teacher is perceptive, he may help the child unearth talents he did not know he possessed.

Try to understand your troubled child. He may live in a world so different from yours that the bridges are indeed few. But construct not one but several—for only if you can enter his universe, only if you are able to cross over into his realm will he ever be able to enter yours. Whether he is handicapped by poverty or by physical condition, he is still far, far away. Try to draw him close to you, for then, and only then, will you be able to teach him.

TWELVE

The Drug Abuser and the Child Who Drinks (Intoxicating Beverages)

One of the most serious, and one of the most tragic, problems facing the youth of the entire world today is the drug menace—a threat not only to adolescents, but to younger children as well. Drug abusers are found in all age groups, in every area of the world and in every strata of society. In thinking about drugs we must remember that there is a veritable well of riches in the medicine chest of virtually every middle-class, and many lower socio-economic homes—that drug abuse involves pills of all variety and potency. Marijuana, heroin and LSD are well known—but amphetamines and barbiturates are used, too (the so-called ups and downs); even glue or cleaning fluid may be sniffed by children looking for some sort of experience, usually a "high" brought on by artificial stimuli. The child who takes drugs may be a discipline problem because of talkative, boisterous behavior, or he may be withdrawn and "out of it," confined to his own private world.

There are, too, a large number of children who drink alcoholic beverages. They are most frequently found in the high schools, but occasionally in the junior high and elementary school, as well. They may be "high," too, or sleepy, depending, of course, on what they have been drinking. However, beer and wine are not at all

181

unusual, and pint bottles of scotch and rye have been confiscated from "little" girls and boys in the seventh and eighth grade.

Alcoholism has been considered one form of drug abuse, the drug abused, of course, being alcohol. Surely it is obvious a great many aspects of these problems are of similar nature, and so are considered together in this chapter. Our purpose, as it has been throughout this book, is to show how you, the teacher, can help your children when they are troubled—but in the case of either drug or alcohol addiction time is of the essence. We firmly believe that in many cases, experimentation with one drug leads to further experimentation, and it is fervently desired that this be prevented. If you suspect a child is taking any drug, start work with that youngster immediately by referring the case to the proper authority within your school. It may be the principal, his assistant, the guidance counselor or a designated teacher—but the referral should be made as quickly as possible. Then work with the child yourself. First, let us consider the type of child who gets involved in this kind of behavior.

The Underlying Inadequate Personality—or the Experimenter

The child who takes alcohol or drugs is very often the one who cannot cope with the problems presented by the world around him—be they in school or at home. Because he is unhappy, because he cannot face the trials and tribulations the day brings, because he may be bored or unhappy and seeks a "lift," he needs some external stimulation—and he finds it in pills or pot, a shot or a swig.

However, there are other children, too, who take drugs—or use alcohol for a much more superficial reason. They are talked into experimentation, or they try them because "everyone is doing it." It takes an extremely strong person to be able to reject an activity which his peers are pushing. Years ago it was smoking cigarettes which some youngsters would reject; today it's smoking pot. The need to be "one of the fellas" is uppermost in many young people's minds, and will supersede any misgiving they may have about trying drugs. What is worse, to a youngster, than being called "chicken"? So many children will take any chance rather than be rejected by their classmates or playmates.

Recognizing the Various Types of Drug Abuse

The table (Illustration 1) is the Drug Abuse Products Reference Chart. We suggest you study it carefully, for the information contained may be of great help to you, the teacher. Glue sniffing, we know, is very common among elementary and junior high school children because the glue is readily obtainable. Far, far more of it is sold for this purpose than for its legal one—making model airplanes. Other chemicals, such as carbon tetrachloride, a common cleaning fluid, are used for the same purpose. One young lady in the sixth grade, a perfectly behaved child, when asked why she had sniffed glue, answered, "I broke up with my boy friend, and I just couldn't face the day without sniffing." It was discovered, however, that she was not alone. Three of her friends joined her— and they said they had been doing this every day for a month because it "made them feel good." This brings up the tremendous need for education—of even very young children, in regard to the dangers inherent in the use of any chemical or drug when it is not prescribed by a physician. These young ladies were shocked to learn of the potential brain damage which often results from glue sniffing.

The drugs found in the home—and there are many, which can be abused—range from cough medicine to diet pills. Should you have a child in your class who is behaving peculiarly, observe him carefully. Very often drug users will lose interest in their school work, and will show other behavioral changes. Apathy sets in. Their clothing and appearance may deteriorate. (Do not confuse this with current styles, however.) There are many, many signs of abuse—drunken appearance, stupor, drowsiness or dazed appearance. Just the opposite, too, may be true—a lack of coordination, aggressive behavior, giggling or excessive talking.

If you believe a child has taken any drug, we have one suggestion. Have the child write a paragraph. It is a good idea to assign this to the entire class, to avoid singling out the youngster. If the youngster you suspect is really under the influence of some drug he often cannot write—will produce "chicken tracks." If you get these scrawls, you have almost positive proof. If the child can write, he may still have taken something, but you have no proof in either direction.

DRUG ABUSE PRODUCTS REFERENCE CHART

NAME	SLANG NAME	CHEMICAL OR OFFICIAL NAME	SOURCE	HOW TAKEN WHEN ABUSED	USUAL FORM OF PRODUCT	EFFECTS SOUGHT	LONG-TERM POSSIBLE EFFECTS
MORPHINE	WHITE STUFF, M.	MORPHINE SULPHATE	NATURAL (FROM OPIUM)	SWALLOWED OR INJECTED	POWDER (WHITE) TABLET LIQUID	EUPHORIA, PREVENT WITHDRAWAL DISCOMFORT	ADDICTION, CONSTIPATION, LOSS OF APPETITE
HEROIN	H, HORSE, SCAT JUNK, SMACK, SCAG STUFF, HARRY	DIACETYL-MORPHINE	SEMI-SYNTHETIC (FROM MORPHINE)	INJECTED OR SNIFFED	POWDER (WHITE GRAY, BROWN)	EUPHORIA, PREVENT WITHDRAWAL DISCOMFORT	ADDICTION, CONSTIPATION, LOSS OF APPETITE
CODEINE	SCHOOLBOY	METHYLMORPHINE	NATURAL (FROM OPIUM, SEMI-SYNTHETIC (FROM MORPHINE)	SWALLOWED	TABLET LIQUID (IN COUGH SYRUP)	EUPHORIA, PREVENT WITHDRAWAL DISCOMFORT	ADDICTION, CONSTIPATION, LOSS OF APPETITE
PAREGORIC		TINCTURE OF OPIUM, BENZOIC ACID AND CAMPHOR	NATURAL AND SYNTHETIC	SWALLOWED OR INJECTED	LIQUID	EUPHORIA, PREVENT WITHDRAWAL DISCOMFORT	ADDICTION, CONSTIPATION, LOSS OF APPETITE
MEPERIDINE		MEPERIDINE HYDROCHLORIDE	SYNTHETIC (MORPHINE-LIKE)	SWALLOWED OR INJECTED	TABLET LIQUID	EUPHORIA, PREVENT WITHDRAWAL DISCOMFORT	ADDICTION, CONSTIPATION, LOSS OF APPETITE
METHADONE	DOLLY	METHADONE HYDROCHLORIDE	SYNTHETIC (MORPHINE-LIKE)	SWALLOWED OR INJECTED	TABLET LIQUID	PREVENT WITHDRAWAL DISCOMFORT	ADDICTION, CONSTIPATION, LOSS OF APPETITE
COCAINE	CORRINE, COKE FLAKE, SNOW GOLD DUST, STAR DUST, BERNICE	METHYLESTER OF BENZOYLECGONINE	NATURAL (FROM COCA LEAVES)	SNIFFED, INJECTED OR SWALLOWED	POWDER (WHITE) LIQUID	EXCITATION	DEPRESSION, CONVULSIONS
MARIJUANA	POT, GRASS, TEA	CANNABIS SATIVA	NATURAL	SMOKED OR SWALLOWED	PLANT PARTICLES (DARK GREEN OR BROWN)	EUPHORIA, RELAXATION, INCREASED PERCEPTION	USUALLY NONE; BRONCHITIS, CONJUNCTIVITIS, PSYCHOSIS POSSIBLE
HASHISH	HASH	CANNABIS SATIVA	NATURAL	SMOKED OR SWALLOWED	SOLID, BROWN TO BLACK, RESIN	RELAXATION, EUPHORIA, INCREASED PERCEPTION	USUALLY NONE; CONJUNCTIVITIS, PSYCHOSIS POSSIBLE
BARBITURATES	BARBS, RED DEVILS, YELLOW JACKETS, PHENNIES, PEANUTS, BLUE HEAVENS, CANDY	PHENOBARBITAL PENTOBARBITAL SECOBARBITAL AMOBARBITAL	SYNTHETIC	SWALLOWED OR INJECTED	TABLETS OR CAPSULES (VARICOLORED)	ANXIETY REDUCTION, EUPHORIA	SEVERE WITHDRAWAL SYMPTOMS; POSSIBLE CONVULSIONS, TOXIC PSYCHOSIS
AMPHETAMINES	BENNIES, DEXIES, HEARTS, PEP PILLS, SPEED, LID PROPPERS, WAKE UPS	AMPHETAMINE DEXTROAMPHETAMINE METHAMPHETAMINE (DESOXYEPHEDRINE)	SYNTHETIC	SWALLOWED OR INJECTED	TABLETS (VARICOLORED) LIQUID POWDER (WHITE)	ALERTNESS, ACTIVENESS	LOSS OF APPETITE, DELUSIONS, HALLUCINATIONS, TOXIC PSYCHOSIS
LSD	ACID, BIG D, SUGAR, TRIPS, CUBES	D-LYSERGIC ACID DIETHYLAMIDE	SEMI-SYNTHETIC (FROM ERGOT ALKALOIDS)	SWALLOWED	TABLETS (VARICOLORED) LIQUID	INSIGHT, DISTORTION OF SENSES, EXHILIRATION	MAY INTENSIFY EXISTING PSYCHOSIS, PANIC REACTIONS
DOM	STP "SERENITY, TRANQUILITY, PEACE"	4-METHYL-2, 5-DIMETHOXY ALPHA METHYL PHENETHYLAMINE	SYNTHETIC	SWALLOWED	TABLETS (VARICOLORED) LIQUID	STRONGER THAN LSD EFFECTS	?
THC		TETRAHYDROCANNABINOL	NATURAL (FROM CANNABIS SATIVA) SYNTHETIC	SMOKED OR SWALLOWED	IN MARIJUANA OR LIQUID	STRONGER THAN MARIJUANA EFFECTS	?
DMT	BUSINESSMAN'S SPECIAL	DIMETHYL-TRYPTAMINE	SYNTHETIC	INJECTED	LIQUID	SHORTER TERM THAN LSD EFFECTS	?
MESCALINE	MESC	3,4,5-TRIMETH-OXYPHENETHYLAMINE	NATURAL (FROM PEYOTE CACTUS)	SWALLOWED	TABLET	SAME AS LSD	?
PSILOCYBIN		3(2-DIMETHYL-AMINO) ETHYL-INDOL-4-OLDIHYDROGEN PHOSPHATE	NATURAL (FROM PSILOCYBE FUNGUS ON A TYPE OF MUSHROOM)	SWALLOWED	TABLET	SAME AS LSD	?
ALCOHOL	BOOZE, JUICE SAUCE	ETHANOL, ETHYL ALCOHOL	NATURAL (FROM GRAPES, GRAINS)	SWALLOWED, OR APPLIED TOPICALLY	LIQUID	SENSE ALTERATION, ANXIETY REDUCTION, SOCIABILITY	TOXIC PSYCHOSIS, ADDICTION, NEUROLOGIC DAMAGE
TOBACCO	FAG, COFFIN NAIL	NICOTINIA TABACUM	NATURAL	SMOKED, SNIFFED, CHEWED	SNUFF, PIPE CUT PARTICLES CIGARETTES	CALMNESS, SOCIABILITY	LOSS OF APPETITE, HABITUATION
GLUE		AROMATIC HYDRO-CARBONS	SYNTHETIC	INHALED	PLASTIC CEMENT	INTOXICATION	IMPAIRED PERCEPTION, COORDINATION, JUDGMENT

Illustration #1.

The Open Discussion of the Effects of Drugs and Alcohol

Because of the spread of this epidemic, we believe drug education should begin with children in the kindergarten. Of course, all of this material must be geared to the child's level of understanding, and must be handled very carefully and deftly.

In the kindergarten and the first year, it would be wise to teach the children not to speak to strangers—*not even to strange children.* If they are approached by someone they do not know, they should run away immediately—and tell their parent or teacher about this person. They must be taught not to accept any gift of any kind, and never, never, never to put anything into their mouths other than food they get at home or which is served to them *by the school personnel in the school lunchroom.* A strong, dramatic appeal should be made to paint an indelible picture in the children's minds, so that "this message will be written forever upon the tablets of their memory."

At this tender age, children are still "with us" enough to be influenced by what we say, and so it is mandatory that we instruct them, that if they suspect any child of taking drugs, it is their solemn duty to quietly tell the teacher of their suspicions. (As children get older, almost all of them will absolutely refuse to do this, and we cannot count on them for any information. There may be a child in the seventh or eighth grade who will "inform" but he is unusual.)

As the children move ahead in school, and their understanding increases, it behooves us to give them as much education as we possibly can in regard to the tragic effects of drug and alcohol abuse. The possible lifetime effects of heroin and LSD are examples of the seriousness of the situation. You may wish to have them bring in newspaper and magazine articles reporting suicides and murders which resulted from their use. As you discuss this with your youngsters, stress the concept that the abuser is really a child in need of help. Teach them, as Hamlet did, that sometimes we must be cruel only to be kind. Hammer away at this, telling your children that "if you really want to be a friend, then the most compassionate thing you can do is tell his parents or his teacher or both, of the situation—so that he may be spared a lifetime of suffering." If your children reject this, tell them to encourage the drug abuser, himself, to reach out for help, because his very life may be in danger.

Above all, bring the discussion of drugs out into the open. Films, speakers, photographs and the television programs which show young people who speak so eloquently of their own misfortunes as drug addicts—all are important influences which you should bring to protect your children.

Let us point out, too, that the "pusher" is often a child himself, and rarely the slouch-hatted male who drives up in a flashy car.

Both teachers and children should be encouraged to write short stories and poems, preferably narrative poems, depicting strongly the tragic results of drug addiction. The following is a simple poem, illustrating this point. We suggest that you read it aloud, with as much sincerity and dramatic power as you can muster. We feel quite sure it will entice and really hold the children's attention. After reading it, discuss it fully with the children. It might be made the nucleus of a class play or the subject for the artists of the class. Posters and pictures illustrating it, with quotations at the bottom of the pictures, would further spread the all important message of the horrors of drug addiction.

The Little Drug Addict

She died, not in a hospital,
With doctors and nurses
    within call,
And Mom at her side, giving
    her all,
To spare her child suffering
    and pain,
And pray heaven that she
    be well again.
No, this is not how she
    died.
She died alone, at the
    top of a cold staircase,
        in the dark,
Alone, and in agony, she died,
Shedding hot tears that
    could not be dried.
And she cried, "O, Mommy,
    Mommy"!
"Forgive me! I trusted a

stranger more than
   I trusted you."
"Mommy, Mommy, please
   help me!
The pain, I can't stand
   the pain!"
But Mom heard her not,
   and found her not.
Though she searched
   everywhere.
"My little girl didn't
   come home last night,"
Said the frantic mother
   to the policeman,
And a sob tore her words
   apart,
As she stood there with
   a breaking heart;
And the kind cop wiped
   away a tear,
As he saw her tremble,
   tremble with fear.
"We have found your little
   girl, my dear."
And the policeman turned
   his head away.
For he could not bear
   to see the mother's face
      twisted in pain;
While he tried to comfort
   her saying,
That her baby would never
   suffer again.
As he spoke the sad
   words,
The mother fell to
   the ground,
When she heard how her
   poor little girl
      had been found.

And that mother knelt
   and prayed for her child
Who had died that day,

And would be buried
in the churchyard,
not far away.
And she added, "Sweet
Heaven, save us all
from such a fate,
As that which befell
My darling,
My darling,
My own little Kate"!

Dark and soft and beautiful
Had been the little girl's
eyes.
In school she had won
many a prize;
For often a sweet song
she would write and sing.
What pleasure to Mother
and teacher and friends
she could bring!
But sing and write she
would no more
Words and notes that flowed
from her tender heart's
core,
For these gentle eyes
were closed forevermore.

Asleep in the churchyard
near the countryside,
By her own small hand
Our little girl died.

Many teachers have children writing poems about sunshine,
and flowers or the autumn or the spring. Let us, for the moment,
forget about these beauties, and write, instead about the all-important subject of drug addiction.

A class poem is particularly effective, with all the children par-
ticipating. You will find the youngsters will stimulate each other.
The teacher must be very skillful in supplying a word or a phrase.
It is his enthusiasm that will carry this project through.

Why Oh Why?

By Felice Schoenbrun

Why oh why?
Do people cry?
When they see their children in trouble.
They think of the problems that could be double.
When the children raise their mugs.
Or go on drugs.
So let us all win.
By stopping this terrible sin.

Illustration #2.

Becoming a Friend Must Be the First Step

The teacher must never sit in judgment upon any child. On the contrary, he should be the shield protecting the child from pernicious influences. By his manner, his actions and his words, he must convey to the child that he is his friend—that he really cares about him, and that his one and only intention is to help him. As we have said, the drug abuser or alcohol abuser is generally an unhappy child, trying to make life livable for himself. Sometimes a teacher does offer friendship, and the offer is not accepted. This often comes as a distinct shock to the adult. Yet the child is a very troubled child. The teacher should continue, with his eyes upon the child, to convince him that he really wants to help. The French have a saying which is very appropriate to this situation—"Tout comprendre c'est tout pardonner."—"To understand all is to forgive all."

However, the teacher must call the situation to the attention of the administration so that help may be obtained. This, too, presents difficulty, for the child may feel he is being betrayed. This requires a great deal of deftness on the part of the teacher.

"Billy," he says, "we must get some help for you right now. You realize, don't you, that your life may be in danger. But if we can help you immediately, you can be spared misery, suffering or even death." This type of conversation is exceedingly difficult—requiring the teacher to muster all the eloquence which his sincerity will lend him. For what he is saying is absolutely true. How often have we read in the newspapers or seen on the television screen that a pill swallower has taken an overdose that resulted in death!

Referring the Child, While Working with the Parents

As soon as the parents have been informed, the teacher may be able to do a great deal to help the parent, as well as the child. He should do everything he can to encourage the parent to contact the right social agencies—where assistance can be obtained. Remember to stress the importance of time element—and that action be taken immediately so that tragedy be averted.

The teacher is in a position to befriend the child by telling the parents of the youngster's good qualities—which will help him combat the pernicious habit. There are those parents who will throw up their hands and disown their children. Unfortunately this is all too common. It is with this type of parent that the teacher must leave no stone unturned to convince that help is obtainable, and not to feel desperate about the situation. Drug abuse has been and can be conquered in a great number of cases—depending in a large measure on the help the parents obtain for the child. There may not be an agency in the immediate community, but by consulting the guidance counselor or the administration, one can be located. But, again, remember! time is of the essence.

The Pleas for Understanding

You, the teacher, may have to plead very strongly with parents on behalf of the child. Often this youngster has already been in difficulty, and the parents are annoyed.

Let us consider Randy. At the tender age of 15, she has been taking various types of pills for two years. She is lethargic about herself—her appearance showing a total lack of interest. Her schoolwork is virtually nil. She does, however, carry an armload of books.

An interview with the parent discloses the total lack of communication between child and parent. Frequently, even so harsh a phrase as "Don't bother me," has been said by the mother to the girl, when the child wants to talk to her.

The family is on welfare, and there are five children. The mother is very quick to tell the listener.that Randy has always caused her trouble. "My other four are so good," she announces. "I don't know what's the matter with this one. What can I do"? When told, Randy's mother does not bother to follow through. Even when informed the child is a drug abuser, she is not willing to face up to this serious situation. Her tendency is to sweep it under the rug.

It then behooves the teacher to show her the great need the child has for her mother's understanding and help at this crucial time in order that the child might be given a chance to be cured of this tragic habit. The child does wish to gain her mother's approval. The large number of books she carries is indicative of this wish to impress the parent. She needs much help—of a professional nature. However, if this mother can be made to see how really vital her role is, she can be the main instrument in saving the child from becoming an addict. The teacher's forcefulness in speaking to the mother is all-important. If you are placed in such a position, speak with your heart.

The Bridging of the Generation Gap Is a Must— and the Bridge Is Love

All human beings need to be respected. There is no child, regardless of age, who does not long for recognition. He wishes his opinions to be heard and his voice, his presence, his ideas to carry some weight. In the classroom, we must make him feel he is an important person, lest he seek other companionship, and other "teachers" who will make him feel "like a big shot," and possibly ensnare him with flattery. Should these be pernicious persons, they might seriously damage the child's personality and character, for it is in just these situations that drug addicts come into being.

We must either preclude their becoming involved or if they are already involved, we must wean them away. This is particularly true when "teachers" are their peers.

The situation is a very delicate one, for young children are "with us." They trust us—and it is not hard to gain their confidence. However, as most of them reach their teens, the tendency is to band together, exchanging confidences with their peers, rather than with their parents and teachers. Never, but never ask a child to inform. If you can create a warm, confidential atmosphere, perhaps the child will bring to you information which may save him or his friends, or both, from disaster. Here again, the ingenuity and warmth of the teacher is the keynote. You must never insult or belittle a child. Whatever error he may have perpetrated, belittling or insulting him will accomplish less than nothing. Try to win him to your side. At the teen age this is exceedingly difficult, but if treated with love and respect, you can win even these children over. This is what we mean by bridging the generation gap with love.

Educating All of the Children to See the Danger of Abusing Drugs

There is no teacher who can ignore the deep importance of preventing the use of drugs, when we consider that addicts have been found—even among the little seven-year-olds. Every teacher should have a program of some sort dealing with the misuse of drugs. Education is the only way to arrest the epidemic among the young, and it is education on a day-to-day basis. Frankly, openly and fearlessly the teacher must combat it. The arts are her allies— pictures, stories, anecdotes, plays, films. Find those which deal potently with the subject. The topic can and should be brought into any and every subject area. The children are extremely involved in this problem. It is almost as if it is their own. It has become the fairyland of the child of this generation. We have seen a noisy class come to order instantaneously when the topic is brought to their attention. We had an audience of 500 children waiting for a film on this topic to start. The person in charge tried to quiet them. "Don't bother," the speaker said, "As soon as we begin showing the film, you'll be able to hear a pin drop." It was uncanny how quickly the auditorium became silent.

Older children are getting some work in this field. Younger children need it too, in larger measures, if we are to believe the "ounce of prevention is worth a pound of cure."

If you have a child in your class who is taking drugs, gear your lessons to convincing him of the serious consequences of his acts. Do not sit in judgment upon him, lest you alienate him. Rather make him feel that you are his friend in need—for this is the only way you can possibly reach him and obtain the assistance for him that may lead to his cure.

If a child has never been told, how is he to learn about overdosing? This is particularly important if he is small, and light in weight, because the amount of drug a person can tolerate safely is determined by his body weight. How is he to learn of the danger of buying drugs, and taking them—when they may have had added to them strychnine or rat poison? How is he to learn this dangerous fact unless we teach it specifically to him. Forewarned is forearmed!

Each teacher should be knowledgeable in these matters—never exaggerating or making overstatements—but being very factual in the teaching of this subject, for there is nothing so convincing and so potent as the truth. Teenagers in particular feel they "know it all," and if you tell them something they believe is untrue, they will pay no attention whatsoever to whatever else you say. Adults, for example, will list all of the "dangers" of marijuana—yet at the time of this writing, the research is inconclusive. There is, however, one fact which is undeniable—that smoking "pot" is against the law. This type of information which we must give them—if we are to avoid a credibility gap—and a credibility gap is something we must avoid if we possibly can. We must use objective material —facts—which the youngsters will respect, and we must always listen carefully, and patiently, to every statement any child has to say on the subject. If we are to win his confidence, we must make him feel we respect his opinions, or he will shut his mind to our teachings.

Dramatic Education

When you have children who are drug abusers, you might wish to consider taking them to places such as the morgue or to psychiatric wards of hospitals, where they will see sad object lessons of child drug abuse. However, before you do this, make the trip yourself to be sure the desired effect will be produced. We have, for instance, seen young people dead of overdoses—really horrible to behold. But we have visited rehabilitation centers where the surroundings are so pleasant (and this is no exaggeration) children could desire being placed in them—particularly those youngsters coming from broken homes, or from deplorable physical conditions. The teacher must use judgment and discretion. A similar warning should be in effect in regard to inviting into the school, as speakers, so-called ex-addicts. We know of instances when they have become heroes for the children, glamorous figures, "with a fascinating past." This may prove to be risky business, and we feel caution must be taken to be sure the children don't decide to follow in these young people's footsteps. Then, too, the rate of cure for heroin addicts is very low—and an ex-addict today may be a user again tomorrow. Giving him the opportunity to become friendly with children in school can set up a potentially dangerous situation, particularly if these children have been experimenting on their own. It is far safer to show films, have panel discussions and involve your local Police Department in your program.

Keeping the Means of Communication Open

The drug abuser is usually a child who desperately needs friends. If he will allow you to be his ally, please take the opportunity. Talk to him privately, and try to develop a relationship with him. You may find yourself rebuked—or virtually ignored. Never take this personally. Instead, assure the child, "I am your friend, and I am honestly interested in you. Whenever you need me—I shall try to help you." We have seen children return to see teachers years later as a result of such conversations. (Of course you would never make such statements if you did not mean them.)

Some children too often get the feeling, "No one gives a damn about me." It is terribly hard to reach them—but these are the ones who desperately need you. Their lack of self-esteem may be reflected in their dependence on drugs, or in other patterns of behavior, but if you can show them you care—there is always a chance you can be of real assistance to them at some time. The words we have suggested are simple—almost obvious, but it's tragic how rarely they are said, especially to the child who needs to hear them—because he is physically dirty or unattractive—because he is uncommunicative, or because he has so many problems. Even if you feel your words are not being heard or accepted, say them anyway. Keep the lines of communication open—on your end, at least.

Children Who Drink

There is some question as to which it is easier to obtain—drugs or alcohol. Sadly, both are readily accessible to young people. We know of one shop where a 14-year-old could easily purchase wine. Liquor was a bit more difficult. Most of the young people who drink start with wines—because they are relatively inexpensive. A case in point:

Stanley, a tall, handsome boy had a good word for everyone. He would smile, pleasantly, as he greeted people in the hallways. He was constantly wandering. Of course, he should have been in class, but he chose not to attend whenever the desire to cut came over him. He was a joker, a Puckish character, but he was failing every subject at the end of the first marking period. A meeting with Stanley and his mother was arranged. As we sat around the table, the boy's expression was completely different. He was not smiling. The conference was eminently successful. Stanley stopped missing classes. His work improved. But he no longer smiled. While behaving civilly, he was certainly not pleasant. One day in the hall, one of Stanley's friends was overheard to comment, "How he has changed—since he stopped having a bottle of wine for breakfast"!

It is as important for us to teach our children about alcohol abuse as it is to teach the effects of drug abuse. Alcohol is still believed to be more prevalent than narcotics. Furthermore, the number of serious accidents occuring when the drivers are intoxicated is extremely large. If we can get our children to be aware of the effects, and the habit-forming nature of alcohol, we are doing meaningful teaching—in terms of an entire lifetime.

If you have a child in your class who drinks, make sure the parents are made aware of the situation. Be certain you have proof, however, of any statements you make, for often these parents will become extremely defensive.

Try, in this case, too, to communicate with the child—for he, too, you will usually find, is a lonely person—in need of a friend. As with drugs, he is using alcohol as a means of escape or as a device to prove he is "one of the boys." If you can find out what is causing the child to drink, perhaps this can help you to help him avoid the situation in the future.

It is important that alcohol users be referred both to the guidance counselor and to the principal. The problem is no less acute than drug-abuse. Parents must be interviewed, and steps taken to prevent the child from buying or "finding" the liquor. (How many parents lock up their liquor supply?) If there is a shop in the community which sells wine or whiskey to your youngsters or any persons below the legal age, it should be referred to the police department—for this is, of course, against the law.

In any discussion, be extremely careful you do not pass value judgments on the adult user of alcohol. It is necessary to discourage children from its use, but being careful not to condemn the adult—particularly the "social drinker." We know of one case where an alert seven-year-old told her teacher, "My father drinks." "Oh, no," said the teacher. "I know your father. He certainly doesn't drink." "Yes he does," insisted the child. Then she added, "Every year on the holidays he drinks part of a cup of wine. I saw him!" Surely many children have seen the results of alcohol abuse on the streets and in public places, but, should there happen to be a member of the family so afflicted, it is important that the child not be embarrassed. Nevertheless, the problem-drinker should be discussed, in the hope of discouraging the children from even experimenting with alcoholic beverages while they are still children.

CONCLUSION

The drug abuser is a troubled child in the truest sense of the word. While he may be involved in experimenting with relatively less harmful drugs now, there is always the chance he will go on to LSD or hashish, to heroin or cocaine. For this reason, should you discover him using any drug, you must take immediate action—by notifying the proper authorities within the school, and by communicating with the parents. The same procedures should be taken with the child who drinks alcoholic beverages, for this is just as serious a problem.

After notifying the authorities and the parents, however, you will still have the child in your class. Make sure that you have warned him before-hand that you had to notify the principal and his family so that you are not doing anything "behind his back." As long as he is your pupil, you must treat him with care, showing him respect and understanding. You must try to keep the lines of communication between you open, for, by so doing, it is possible that you can help him with his problems. Remember he is a sick child—with the ever-present possibility he may become even sicker.

Drug abuse is an affliction of the young, for the most part. Alcoholism is a scourge at any age. It is surely then up to us, as teachers, to help eliminate these afflictions, as we try to eradicate the others—ignorance, bigotry and poverty. If you are able to help any child to conquer or to preclude these dreadful habits of drug abuse or alcoholism, what greater service can you possibly render?

THIRTEEN

The Seriously Disturbed Child

Probably the most serious problems you will face in your teaching career are those dealing with the seriously disturbed children. These are the ten percent of our population whom it is conjectured will spend some time during their lives in mental institutions. (However, with the advent of new medication, it is possible that, happily, this may not come to pass.) But in the classroom, these are your "impossible children," the ones you cannot understand.

Recognizing the Child Who Is Really Disturbed

How can you recognize these children? Often they perform bizarre acts which you realize immediately are "way out." "This child is out of his mind," you think. "He's crazy." And, unfortunately, you are probably right. But he is in your class, and you must cope with him—and help him to adjust to the school situation—if it is at all possible.

When you have a child whose actions are very different from

198

those of normal children, you may suspect that he is seriously disturbed. (Incidentally, genius, too, may display eccentric behavior, but it will be quite obvious to you that this is a child of unusual intellectual ability and his actions, while unusual, will not be destructive.)

Let us discuss some cases, which, while they are comparatively rare, are still seen in many classrooms, when the entire school population is considered. We have known children, for example, who claim they talk to God and are answered. One such young lady would recount long stories about her conversations—she was constantly asking for forgiveness, and it would be an agonizingly long time for her before it was granted. Yet the actions for which she asked to be pardoned were events of everyday living—"little white lies," for instance. This is, of course, paranoic behavior. Other youngsters may hear voices, or hallucinate, and these children are generally very seriously disturbed.

Another form of paranoia is illustrated by the child who complained to his teacher, "They're after me." "Everyone in this class hates me." When questioned, he admitted every boy and girl he knew felt the same way about him. These feelings of persecution make it difficult for the child to function in a class situation. He may fight these "enemies," or hide from them, but enemies they are—to his disturbed mind.

Climbing is normal for young children, but, in a playground situation, not a classroom. Witness the seventh grader who crawled along the lighting fixtures, and on the window sills, laughing uproariously as he went. The child who completely isolates himself, while not usually a discipline problem, should still be considered as a sick child. Very often he appears angry if his classmates even approach him.

One of the saddest cases we ever worked with was a teen-age girl, who, at times, would place her chair in a corner of the classroom, and suck her thumb. If other children spoke to her, she used extremely foul language in reply. She paid no attention to the teacher's words when she was behaving this way, and, in fact responded in the same manner to her. On other days she would be pleasant and would really try to cooperate. One day the girls in her class ran screaming to the teacher in charge. They were in the cafeteria, a huge room, with hundreds of children. "Look at Mildred, look at Mildred," they shrieked. And the sight was unbelievable for this poor sick child had permitted her menstrual blood to cover her chair, and her skirt. She was happily parading around, almost proud of herself.

When a child's actions are so out of the ordinary, consider then, that there is a very strong possibility that he or she may be mentally disturbed.

Bizarre Acts, and How to Handle Them

What do you do if you have a child who behaves in such a manner?

1) Check his records to see if there is previous behavior of similar nature. Very often you will find there is.

2) Speak to previous teachers, asking them if incidents occurred in their classes—and if so, *how did they handle them?* This can be most helpful. We know of youngsters who cannot be screamed at. If a teacher raises his voice to such a child, an altercation is sure to occur. The child must be spoken to in a very soft voice, instead.

3) After an incident, when the youngster has calmed down, talk to him quietly, asking him, "Johnny, why did you do that"? Give him a chance to explain to you, but then say softly and gently to him, "We have a rule. You cannot do this! It endangers you—and other members of the class. You cannot break the rules. Promise me you will try not to."

Understand he probably cannot help himself, but make him aware of the rules, and keep referring to them. Stress fairness—in a word, that the rules apply to everybody.

4) Send notes to the guidance counselor, and to the principal. This makes the administration aware, as it should be, of possible future serious problems. If these never come to pass, fine. But, if they do light has already been thrown upon "the case."

One teacher sent the following note, "I've noticed Jim Jones likes to light matches. I found him playing with a package, which I confiscated." Several weeks later there was a fire in the boys' bathroom. Jim was, of course, suspect—and when a number of children were questioned, his guilt was established. It had been the teacher's short note which alerted the administration to the guilty party.

5) Discuss the child's behavior with the guidance counselor. Because he may know the youngster he may have suggestions. He

may also know if the child has been under psychiatric treatment. There are sometimes a surprisingly large number of children receiving such assistance in a school.

6) After the second incident, (or even the first if it was serious) write the parents a note, or phone them setting up an interview. Try to learn from them if the child behaves unusually at home. Some parents may not be quite open with you, but others may— and the information they have to offer may be of great help. Particularly, try to find out if the child has been seen by a psychiatrist, a psychiatric social worker, or has been in any sort of therapy.'

7) Be fair, but be firm with this type of child. He needs to know the rules of acceptable behavior. Tell him, for example, you will have to be in touch with his parents whenever he steps out of line. Tell him he will lose his monitorial status if he repeats his previous behavior. Try not to lose your patience—but let him know there are limits he cannot ignore. And never threaten to do anything you cannot do.

8) Whenever you have a serious behavior problem in your class, take the other children into your confidence. This is most effectively done when the troubled child is absent. You may say to the children, "We all realize that Mary's behavior is often very unusual. I know each of you is interested in helping her, and me, and all the rest of us. By being friendly to her, and by trying to understand her, perhaps you can get her to see that the rules we make are for the benefit of everyone—including Mary, and that it is necessary for her welfare, and everyone's, that these rules be obeyed."

Add very fervently, "I think you children can do more than I can to help her." We guarantee you, in the light of our many years of experience as teachers, that the children will be willing and eager to help you. We have seen cooperation "above and beyond," in just these circumstances.

The Frustrations of Working with Seriously Disturbed Children

Have you ever felt you are taking two steps forward, and then three back? The feeling of frustration is utterly depressing. So it is when you work with the seriously disturbed child. You talk to him, you reason, you do not lose your patience. You even grow to love the child. And then, like a bolt from the blue, he's at it again. He screams invectives at you—when all you did was ask him to sit down and do his work.

What should you do? Wait until he has calmed down. Speak to him very quietly. If he is agitated, think of a quiet place out of the classroom, and take him to it *yourself.* (Leave the class president in charge.) If you can control yourself, don't scream. Don't try recriminations—at this time. Later on, when the child is calm, speak to him. Invariably he will say to you, "I couldn't help it." And the truth of the matter is, he really can't. We have heard this statement hundreds of times. To a person who has control of his actions, it is awfully difficult to fully comprehend it. But if you consider the child ill, perhaps the concept is easier to grasp.

Julie was a lovely girl—lovely to look at—so that it came as a distinct shock when children reported she bit them for absolutely no reason. She loved to swing her handbag—hard. It always made contact with another child's anatomy—usually a girl, and usually her head. (One term she broke six handbag handles.)

Her teacher questioned her, talked to her, listened to her. One day Julie said, "I like you a lot. If I could stop myself, I would. But I just can't. I just can't help it"!

The most you can ask of a seriously disturbed child is that he try; that he try to obey the rules; that he can please you if he tries. And don't expect more—for you will be doomed to disappointment. Your task is to teach this child—but if he has his own demons, your task is surely made infinitely more difficult. Your course is to proceed from day to day—accomplishing as much as you can, without becoming frustrated yourself. This is, indeed, uphill work.

The Difficulty of Communication

There are some seriously disturbed children who are very verbal, and who communicate very easily. Others, and this has frequently been our experience, seem to have difficulty speaking— and are leery—and afraid to tell you too much almost for fear of giving themselves away. However, establishing rapport with them is almost essential to their functioning in your classroom.

We have already mentioned the value of having your children write an autobiography for you. It will most assuredly be a help with these troubled children. However, be sure you do not single out any child by requesting that he be the only one who writes it. Read the disturbed child's autobiography carefully and you may then use it as a point of departure to involve the child in conversation.

Be careful, though, not to make value judgments. One normal, healthy child actually wrote the following as part of his autobiography, "I love to go with my parents when they visit cemeteries." (And this was actually where the family did go—when they sought an outing.) Try not to show shock or surprise. It entered the teacher's mind while reading that page to say, "Why on earth do you go to cemeteries? How horrible"! Fortunately she restrained herself. The child's next remark was a telling one. "We live right near this big cemetery—and it's like a nice park. There are no parks where we live." Let us hasten to add, neither the child nor the parents were disturbed.

Telling uncommunicative children about yourself is a good icebreaker. Be careful, though, that you do not say anything which does not bear repetition—for what you say will very probably be repeated—sometimes far and wide. Talking about your interests and hobbies can prove of interest to the youngster. If you can find a common interest—a meeting of the minds, this can be a great help. We know of one teacher who used his tropical fish to reach a very difficult child. He became interested in the care of these fish, and the teacher wisely placed the class aquarium under his care. The threat to remove him from this position of importance helped keep the boy on an even keel for most (but not all) of the school year.

Refer the Child to the Guidance Department Immediately

Whenever a child exhibits strange or unusual behavior, discuss the case with the guidance counselor. The counselor is trained to identify serious problems, and to refer them to the appropriate agencies for assistance. The counselor is able to work with the child, on either a temporary or permanent basis, and to develop a one-to-one relationship with the child. It may be necessary, too, to remove the child from the classroom at times, and one method for doing this is to send him to the counselor's office. This, however, should be done only with the counselor's permission.

The Importance of Early Identification

It is often possible that youngsters who are seriously disturbed may be helped through various forms of psychotherapy. However, these youngsters must be identified, first. Parents, of course, are the logical persons to see such illness, but are too often ashamed to admit it and to seek help. The teacher is next in line. It is his task to refer the child to the guidance department, (or, if there is none, to the administration)—as we have suggested. The teacher, however, should not be the person to suggest any sort of help because it may be bitterly resented and set up barriers to teaching the child. A parent may respond to a teacher's comment with "You think my child is crazy," and get furious. Furthermore, teachers usually do not have an adequate background in psychology or guidance to make judgments, but surely they should discuss problem children with the school's personnel trained in this area.

After a child is referred to a counselor, he may be sent by the latter for special testing to determine the seriousness of his behavior problems. There are a number of tests used for this purpose. However, the teacher is in the front line in spotting the seriously disturbed child. For example, if you notice a youngster who draws knives or weapons, or exhibits any of the patterns we have mentioned in this chapter, keep a watchful eye on him, and refer him for guidance.

Working with the Child in the Classroom

Here are some suggested techniques which may be of help to you in your classroom:

1) Separate seriously disturbed children from other behavioral problems—or from children who are easily led. By changing everyone's seats frequently you can arrange to seat your troubled children among those who will pay them a minimum amount of attention. Often the immediate environment stimulates the seriously disturbed child, and a change can work wonders—for a short time.

2) Give these children a great deal of work—but work which

they can handle and which they enjoy doing. Consider all of the child's abilities and, if you are able to, utilize them. But any child can draw posters—and will feel satisfaction if they are exhibited. Find topics the youngster is interested in—and help him make dioramas illustrating them. We don't know why children are fascinated with prehistoric life, but dinosaurs are as real to them as elephants—and lots more interesting.

Often a disturbed child enjoys working with his hands—doing painting or carpentry. Every youngster can have fun with clay but perhaps it will serve as an outlet for the disturbed child's emotional strains. Working with one's hands is considered to be highly therapeutic.

Making papier-mâché requires tearing up newspaper. If you have a child who needs such activity, because he is upset, have him actually make confetti sized bits—if he wants to. Other youngsters will prefer doing calculations—adding, subtracting, multiplying, or dividing. If a child gets satisfaction from doing them—fine. Still others derive comfort from penmanship drills. This is almost a lost practice—but can prove a valuable one.

Oftentimes the disturbed child who has a talent with words will find an outlet in a stream of consciousness kind of writing. He writes his agitation out of his system, so to speak. He is, to quote the Bard, "unpacking his heart with words."

3) Physical education is valuable, too, providing the class does not become over-stimulated. Baseball and volleyball can provide fun—and serve as an emotional outlet for many children. Simple calisthenics can be done in the classroom. Be sure every child has medical permission for this.

4) If you wish, you may give a seriously disturbed child a daily report card to have signed by his parents—and which you sign each day. This keeps the family informed of the child's actions from day to day—so that should the youngster have to be removed from school, the parents cannot claim they were not notified. However, be sure this report is truthful—for if your comments do not reflect the actual situation, they are of little value. As is very often the case, a seriously disturbed child may have one serious incident and then may appear to have been transformed. If he has been, that is truly wonderful. However, several months later another outburst may occur. Unless the parent is informed by you, he will never hear about it. He thinks his child is "doing fine"—and if serious action must be taken by the school he is

shocked by it. He is entitled to be informed—and your doing so is an important part of your work.

5) Record keeping.

Keeping an anecdotal record of the behavior of the seriously disturbed child is the task of the teacher in the elementary school. If the youngster is in junior high or high school, the home room teacher may do it. This record, however, may be kept, instead, by the dean of discipline, by an administrator or by the guidance department. It is essential, though, that someone keep it—for without such a record, it is often impossible to exclude a very ill child from school.

The guidance department should be kept informed too, for, hopefully, the counselor is working with the child, and with the family, as well.

6) We have previously discussed developing a success pattern, and it is in no situation more important than with the troubled child. His self-esteem may sorely need nourishment—and development. Find jobs he can do, give him work which you can subsequently exhibit, and you may see vast improvement in his behavior.

7) Watch, watch, watch.

If you have a seriously disturbed child in your class, try to watch him. Of course you cannot possibly have your eyes on him all the time, but it is well worth scheduling your time so that you have as little clerical work to do as possible while the children are in your room. We have found that relatively few serious incidents occur when the teacher is actively supervising the lesson. He may not be actually speaking but his watchful eye can prevent many outbreaks, particularly by disturbed children.

One teacher saw a youngster take a knife from his pocket, open it and place it inside his desk. But he did not see this action by chance. He always kept his eyes on this boy—for this youngster had given many clues to the seriousness of his problems. The teacher quietly took the knife, telling the boy to see him after class. He then discussed the school's rules in regard to knives—and told the child to have his mother come in to school to get it. Of course the child never delivered the message. Perhaps he forgot. He was only in the second grade.

8) Remember, many seriously disturbed children have very short attention spans. It is exceedingly difficult to keep them interested for long periods of time. However, you might wish to try

some sort of programmed material with them. It is not essential to purchase expensive equipment to do this. There are a number of products available, in form similar to workbooks, which might prove of value. Even the conventional type of workbook can be useful—if used judiciously—for short periods of time.

9) If a child in your class has been seen by a physician and tranquilizers have been prescribed, the task of making sure he takes them may very well fall to you. Far too often these very effective pills may remain at home, in a drawer, where they do the child little or no good. If you are sure they have been prescribed, ask the parent if he would like you to see to it that Johnny takes his pills. If his response is affirmative, very quietly arrange to say to Johnny, "It's time for your pill," or "It's time for you to go to the office for me." The latter is a signal, which might be preferable with a sensitive child.

We were skeptical in regard to the use of tranquilizers, but have seen many children, unable to function without them, do very well when they take them conscientiously. We've even said, "Mary, did you forget to take your medication today"? because the change in Mary's behavior was obvious. They are not the answer to all serious problems, but surely are of great value.

No teacher is in a position to recommend tranquilizers. This recommendation must come from a physician. However, the administration may suggest the parent take the child for a physical examination and explain his behavior to the doctor. Very often it is the medical man who suggests this type of medication.

Make Coming to School a Privilege

Some people believe children would rather stay home than attend school. It has been our experience that this is not true, and that if school attendance is regarded as a privilege rather than forced upon youngsters, they react entirely differently. In the case of the seriously disturbed child, his actions may necessitate suspending him for short periods of time. Often a suspension can be the action which will cause the parents to have the child examined by a physician. On other occasions, parents have been asked to keep the youngster at home. While not a formal suspension, this threat of action may be sufficient to curtail the child's misbehavior. "If he had a cold, you would keep him home, wouldn't you?

Well, he needs a cooling off period—so that he will realize attending school is desirable, and that by his actions he is jeopardizing his right to attend." Unfortunately this is often necessary to protect the other children. No teacher can say this, but administrators can, and at times do, depending on the rules of the school system in which they serve.

We have found that with certain children, this action has a marked favorable effect on their behavior.

Helping the Child to Adjust

Some seriously disturbed children are, almost by definition, unable to adjust to the classroom situation. If you can work with them, helping them to see the reasons for obeying rules, and helping them to alter their behavior to fit into the school's society, you are doing the most effective teaching possible.

For many of these children have never had to live by rules—or have been unable to do so. Their environment has adjusted to them, rather than they to the environment, and, faced with school, they have no background for living by rules.

Learning about a child from his previous teachers and from his parents may be of great help in this area. Developing rapport with the youngster, always important, is even more so with these.

To what, specifically, do we refer when we use the term "adjust"? Adjustment implies cooperation, and consideration of the rights of others. It implies compliance with rules made to protect everyone in the school, and above all it means the ability to show self-control and self-discipline.

Remember, though, that particularly from these sick children, one cannot possibly expect perfection—that all we can ask of them is that they try, that they try again and again, to show self-discipline and self-control.

Learn As Much As You Can About the Seriously Disturbed Child, but Beware of Labels.

A case in point: Jennie had been in four state mental hospitals, for periods of three months to two years. She was considered "disturbed." A very serious child, she rarely smiled, had no friends, and managed to alienate the children in her class by her tough manner of speech. She was placed in a junior high school, but told she could be suspended at any time—if she became involved in any fights. She always managed to avoid them, but she made other youngsters feel uncomfortable. "Yes, ma'am" or "No, ma'am" were her customary responses. She dressed in a manner which was definitely unfeminine, and people were afraid of her for, with her record of hospitalization, it was assumed she was dangerous.

One alert counselor decided to delve deeper into the case. She interviewed the mother, and found her to be a hard, brutal woman who believed children were placed on earth to serve their parents. Since the child's father had deserted her at the time of Jennie's birth, she was terribly bitter in regard to men—and to this daughter, because of her father. The girl was a virtual slave—and she constantly ran away from home. For this, her mother had had her institutionalized four times! Jennie, despite the manner she affected, was not aggressive. The counselor discussed her case with Jennie's teachers, and they changed their attitudes toward her. They were interested and sympathetic and with their help, and the work of the counselor, she, too, changed. She graduated from junior high—and she learned a little about relating to human beings—and trusting them.

Exclusion from School

Many seriously disturbed children, such as a number of those mentioned in this chapter, have proved to be unable to function in a regular school situation, and have had to be placed under home instruction or in special schools. However, this is done only after working with the child, and usually after psychiatric examination. The teacher's role in this is to supply the anecdotal information necessary, showing the child's behavior pattern, and illustrating the problems the child manifests. Each incident should be dated, and, as has been pointed out, the action the teacher took should be noted.

Far too often, before a child is excluded from school, he must perpetrate some drastic misdemeanor, which establishes him as being a seriously disturbed child. Generally it is the culmination of repeated anti-social behavior. It is the signal that our efforts, however great, have been defeated. The loss is ours, as well as the child's.

Prevention

How much better it would be if our combined efforts can serve as preventative medicine that will preclude anti-social behavior that is so often detrimental to the child, and to society, as well. The task of working with disturbed children must fall to everyone —to the youngsters in his class, to the teachers, to the guidance counselors, to the supervisory staff, and to parents and other members of the family. It is possible that someone in the family constellation, other than the parents can affect changes in the child's behavior. It is not terribly important who, specifically, this person is, as long as he can influence the child in the direction of socially acceptable behavior. Very often friends can have an even greater effect on the child's life than adults. A friend will probably be very eager to help—when asked to do so. However, before enlisting his aid, we must be very sure he will be an influence for good, working in the right direction.

CONCLUSION

Working with the seriously disturbed, or mentally ill child is one of the most difficult aspects of our profession. Children who act in bizarre fashion fall into this category.

To work with a child of this type, who may, or may not, try to tear your class apart, find out as much as you can about him— from records, from his previous teachers, from the guidance department, and from his parents. After an incident has occurred, notify the father and mother. In your treatment of the child be firm but be fair. Remember, though, that you cannot expect too much, because, often, the child is incapable of refraining from misbehavior. Try to get through to him, and to establish rapport but do not expect miracles. In the classroom, separate him from other behavioral problems, or from youngsters who are easily led. Find work for him that he will enjoy, and in which he can be successful. You may wish to give him a daily report card but, if you do this, be sure you do not omit incidents of poor behavior, for then you give the parents a false picture of the child's behavior in school.

Keep an anecdotal record of all of the child's activities, so that, should it be necessary to take further action, the principal is able to do so. Keep a watchful eye on this child in order to preclude serious difficulties.

Every avenue of approach should be tried to assist the seriously disturbed child—for, because of the seriousness of his problem, he needs all the help he can get. In school, more than anything else, he needs your patience, your understanding and your affection. Always keep foremost in your mind the fact that this is a sick child, a troubled human being. In the future, he may function in society, or become a burden upon it, depending upon the amount of education he has been able to receive, regardless of his mental illness. We have seen the seriously disturbed child adjust to school, learn, and do well, because of the efforts made by dedicated teachers, who were able to take into consideration the child's strengths as well as his weaknesses, his value to society in spite of his unfortunate handicaps.

FOURTEEN

A Self-Analysis Questionnaire for Every Teacher

The questionnaire which follows requires time and effort to answer, and we are sure you will be able to get an objective picture of your own teaching—of the techniques and methods you use, and of their effect on your children. You will be considering, too, the youngsters' reactions to you as a person, and you to them. When you have completed the questionnaire, you can decide the areas in which you have been remiss and, at a glance, tell which methods you have not tried. You may wish to try them, or you may deem them not worthwhile, but you will have an awareness of the areas in which you are lacking. Your honesty and truthfulness are essential—for, after all, you are doing this for yourself. And for your children.

In Regard to Structuring Your Class Situation

1) In what ways have you indicated to your children what, specifically, you expect of them, in terms of work and in terms of behavior?

2) Have you held class elections, and established specific duties for every class officer?

3) Have you developed, *with the children,* a specific set of rules and regulations for use within their classroom?

4) How have you given the youngsters an awareness of the rules and regulations of the entire school?

5) Have you established a monitorial system—so that every child is a monitor?

6) Have you seated the children—so that each child knows which seat in the classroom is his?

7) Have you seated the children with problems close to you? Have you separated those who tend to talk to one another constantly?

8) Have you reviewed the fire drill procedures—and insisted upon compliance with them?

In Regard to Developing Rapport with Your Children

1) How often do you greet the children with a smile?

2) How often do you engage in small talk with them, or discuss their personal affairs? Is this with the same child, or with different children?

3) How do you encourage children to discuss their problems with you?

4) Do you treat every child the same way? Are there children you allow to do more work for you than others? What is the effect on the other children?

5) In what ways have you attempted to draw out the quiet, retiring child?

6) Do you have a supply of pencils, pens and paper on hand for the children to "borrow?"

7) How often do children stop to talk to you?

8) Many of the children in your class have outside interests— hobbies, jobs, etc. Of how many of these are you aware?

In Regard to the Actual Learning Experiences You Are Giving Your Children

You may wish to check your planbook for answers to the following questions. Another technique is to tape record one of your lessons and review it at your leisure. Best is a combination of the two.

1) How have you linked your lessons with the children's lives? Is there some connection between them—and the lessons you are teaching?

2) Is the technique you used in today's lesson similar to the one you used yesterday? To the one you have planned for tomorrow?

3) Do you lecture?

4) Review several of your lessons. Do they have a variety of experiences within each one?

5) Have you given the children assignments they do "on their own"?

6) Have you discarded any lessons because they do not interest the children?

7) Have you tried to diagnose the skills the children are lacking?

8) Have you taught them those skills—whether they are in reading or math, social studies or penmanship?

9) How have you helped the children develop good work habits?

10) Have you taught your children how to study—actual study skills?

11) Is the pace of your lessons slow or rapid?

12) Are most of the children actively participating most of the time?

13) Have you refused to accept inferior work from any child—or have you settled for it?

In Regard to Teaching Self-Control

1) Do your children feel you can control the class? Do you feel you can?

2) How do you handle children who call out—and are noisy? Do you ignore them? If not, how do you handle the situation?

3) Do you give the youngsters enough work to do—enough to occupy their minds? and hands? How often do you give them a study period?

4) Do you start working immediately or do you wait for the children to get quiet?

5) Do you help the individual child—while the rest of the class is working?

6) Do you set an example by your personal deportment? Do you, for instance, frequently lose your temper?

7) Have you changed the children's seats—so that troublesome children do not sit together?

8) How have you enlisted the aid of the class officers and utilized their services?

In Regard to Developing Rapport with Parents

1) How have you gotten to know them?

2) Have you learned about the special problems the individual child may have?

3) Have you met with the parents, and requested their assistance and cooperation?

4) With how many have you established some parent-teaching program? What success have you had with this?

5) Have you, in conducting parent interviews, approached the parent with some of the good aspects of his child's behavior?

6) How would you approach an irate parent?

7) How would you request an interview?

8) How can you communicate with the parents through the report card?

In Regard to Working with the Troubled or Troublesome Child

1) Have you discussed his behavior with him personally, on a one-to-one basis?

2) Have you tried to show him how his disruptive behavior is wasting valuable class time?

3) Have you tried to determine the specific learning areas in which he is deficient?

4) How have you tried to help him with these?

5) Have you attempted to learn of personal problems he may have?

6) Have you made referrals for guidance or social work?

7) Have you consulted other teachers to try to learn how to "reach" this child?

8) How have you attempted to help this child get a positive image of himself, and his self-worth?

9) Have you tried to get from the child a promise he will try to do his work?

10) In what ways have you shown him warmth and affection? that you care about him?

11) Have you considered the possibility of physical problems affecting the child—and checked into this area?

12) Have you shown your willingness to forgive? After reprimanding a child, how do you show him "bygones will be bygones?"

13) Have you kept notes (from which to write anecdotal records) which can be used to help the child if he needs psychological help?

14) How much do you rely on one child in the class for errands and such work? On several? On the entire class?

15) What specific steps have you taken toward helping the troubled child develop a success pattern?

16) What measures have you taken to supply the hyper-energetic child with work?

17) Have you shown an honest concern for this child and his problems?

Study your answers to these questions; possibly it would help you to imagine them to be the responses of another teacher. Look at them with the viewpoint that perhaps some of the techniques are worth trying, if you have not already done so. Be as objective as you possibly can.

CONCLUSION

No teacher is perfect—as no human being is perfect. But we believe teachers can improve their work, can make great strides forward—for we have seen this happen literally hundreds of times. Far too often the teacher has no concept of where he is going wrong. What mistakes he is making. That is the real purpose of this self-analysis. Make your self-appraisal and, at the same time, get ideas about techniques to try, and methods with which to experiment. You should become a pragmatist, constantly experimenting with new ideas—for this will help you to grow professionally. Without experimentation one stagnates—and if you become bored, the children most assuredly will. The key to teaching is getting and holding the children's interest—but that must include *all* of the children—the troubled as well as the well-adjusted, the slow as well as the bright. The teacher who can interest all of the children and can stimulate them intellectually, artistically and spiritually will have far fewer problems in the classroom. Pupil behavior is poorest where teaching is dullest—in any school, with any child. The time you spend in preparing lessons which the children will enjoy is far more valuable than time spent in disciplining.

With troubled children you must, however, try to extend to them your understanding, help and compassion. For some your classroom must be a refuge from the ills of society—a haven, if you will, from the abuse which can be piled high on them—even at home. When a child lacks self-control, it is your task to determine the cause. If he shouts or punches, if he is playful, or only "fooling around," the reason may be he has not been taught to behave otherwise. You must teach him. If he daydreams, the reason may be the work being done in school holds no importance or interest for him. Whenever there is a child misbehaving, try to find the reason for it.

Most important of all—be the type of person the child will wish to emulate. Far louder than words, your actions indicate what you are as a human being. If you are fair, your children will learn to be fair. If you are cruel or unpleasant, that, too, unfortunately, will be copied. Remember that you are always "on display."

Every educator must be engaged in a never-ending battle. Today, that word is almost forbidden—this being the era of desired love and peace, both of which are devoutly to be wished. But our battle is against ignorance, and against superstition, against fear and against prejudice. These are our enemies. The weapons we use to fight them are compassion and knowledge, love and intellect. And the development of our pupils into thinking, feeling, functioning human beings is the prize we are all fighting for.

And because a troublesome child is so often a troubled child, troubled by a thousand natural and unnatural shocks that he is heir to, the teacher's countenance should be, as was said of Hamlet's father, a countenance more in sorrow than in anger.

Index